COWLEY PUBLICATIONS is a ministry of the brothers of the Society of Saint John the Evangelist, a monastic order in the Episcopal Church. Our mission is to provide books and resources for those seeking spiritual and theological formation. COWLEY PUBLICATIONS is committed to developing a new generation of writers and teachers who will encourage people to think and pray in new ways about spirituality, reconciliation, and the future.

T0149955

The Theological Implications of Climate Control

Reflections on the Seasons of Faith

Brian Erickson

Cowley Publications
Cambridge, Massachusetts

Published in the United States of America by Cowley Publications, a division of the Society of Saint John the Evangelist. No portion of this book may be reproduced, stored in or introduced into a retrieval system, or transmitted, in any form or by any means—including photocopying—without the prior written permission of Cowley Publications, except in the case of brief quotations embedded in critical articles and reviews.

Library of Congress Cataloging-in-Publication Data

Erickson, Brian.
  The theological implications of climate control : reflections on the
seasons of faith / Brian Erickson.
    p. cm.
Includes bibliographical references.
  ISBN 1-56101-227-0 (pbk. : alk. paper)
1. Church year meditations. I. Title.
  BV30.E75 2005
  242'.3—dc22

Scripture quotations are taken from The New Revised Standard Version of the Bible, © 1989, by the Division of Christian Education of the National Council of the Churches of Christ in the United States of America. Used by permission.

Cover design: Gary Ragaglia
Interior design and typesetting: Scribe, Inc. (www.scribenet.com)
This book was printed in the United States of America on acid-free paper.

Cowley Publications
4 Brattle Street
Cambridge, Massachusetts 02138
800-225-1534 www.cowley.org

To Grannie, Papa J, and Henry,
In hope and memory

C ontents

(P)reface

More often than not, those of us who dabble in the theological are looking for ourselves. Most pastors and teachers I know speak of a God who completes them, a Savior who saves them from their own skin. So the quest for God is finally a quest for self. To say one thing about God is to say two things about who we are. Our search declares where we stand, and who we need God to be that day. And conversely, to understand our own souls is to draw nearer to the love of the One who created them.

My on-again, off-again love affair with the church reflects that struggle. At some point in my early teens, I started to realize that my existence was without any kind of real direction. While I was physically in my local church just about every time the doors were open, it seemed that most of the time the folks around me weren't asking the questions of my heart. I was sailing without a compass. For a while, I felt as if I was without past or future—that I was only what I was in that moment—and this awareness, as false as it might have been, filled me with some mixture of joy and sadness. Later I would find out that the confusion of my soul would become the source of a deep and life-giving faith, a faith that looked much different than the shiny, well-put-together piety of many in the communities that raised me. A faith that called me into relationship with a story, a people, and a future.

In those days when I felt as if I had nothing and was nobody, a mentor gently introduced me to the lectionary, a three-year calendar of scripture that tells Christ's story over and over again for the ages. In time, I came to discover that it was also telling *my* story, giving direction and meaning to those haphazard days of self-discovery. I found myself stirring up that dusty road between Nazareth and Jerusalem, alongside a stranger-become-friend. In living alongside the biblical narrative, I discovered that there was also a story inside my skin—a story best understood in light of *the* story.

There are no new words here, no tricks to straighten out your life or understand Leviticus. In fact, if you hear my heart in these pages, you will probably have to disassemble any answers you think you might have. I heard Archbishop Desmond Tutu say once that he only had one sermon, which was basically that God loves us. He felt that until the world understood that first message, he wasn't going to bother coming up with another one. These reflections—centered around accepting the grace of a loving God through a living story—are essentially echoes of the same message, a promise I am still trying to work out for myself. This is an invitation to a journey, to that thin line between chaos and stability that is the only place people of faith will ever feel much at home.

My prayer for you is that somewhere in the ink and paper of these pages, in the tracing of one seeker's journey, you will hear the invitation to walk your own path.

Traveling mercies . . .

Acknowledgments

Up until this point, I've always skipped the acknowledgments page when I'm reading a book, thinking that the book starts when the roman numerals end and the real page numbers begin. But now that I've written one, I realize what a mistake I've been making. This is the heart of the book, the source of the life that's in it. If you're reading this, though, I suppose I'm preaching to the choir.

I read once that good writing is basically an act of hospitality—the best writers recognize that their craft is not necessarily something that springs up from within them, but a holy and fickle visitor. Our work, whether or not we are writers, is to prepare a place for the in-breaking of God. In the precious moments where the words have not been coerced out of my head, I am not sure if the writing is any good, but I am profoundly grateful for the encounter with that sacred visitor.

To have a place to speak and pray and laugh in the language of your heart is also a blessing beyond measure. Those places are few and far between, and they are built not with bricks and capital fund drives, but with the hearts of fellow pilgrims. Almost without exception, these chapters have grown out of my time working with young adults at Birmingham-Southern College, Camp Sumatanga, the University of Evansville, and many points in between. Whatever life is in these words reflects the life of those places. The students I've worked with have been my best preaching professors, holding me accountable to the power of proclamation and often showing me up with their ability to share from the heart. They have also given me the courage to believe these words were worth the paper they're printed on.

My parents have never been less than obnoxiously supportive, even when my calling has pulled me in directions quite different from their own. When I wasn't necessarily following my calling, but testing out the road to nowhere, they waited patiently on the front porch to welcome me home. I hope that I can be as empowering a parent as these two have been to me, allowing my child to grow into the person he is, rather than the one I might want him to be.

This book owes much to my friend, mentor, pastor, colleague, father-in-law, and folk music partner, Stewart Jackson. In a time when I wasn't sure if the church was for me, Stewart took me to the edges of that big tent to show me just how wide the boundaries were, and led me to a place that I could call home. It was his pastoral presence that allowed me to look in the mirror and see myself (with a lump in my throat) as a pastor. It is his grace and gentle encouragement that have given me the space to define that calling for myself, even when my ministry looks much different from his.

My wife, Mollie, helps me to believe that I am lovable, even when that is the hardest thing to believe. Her support for me, her honest critique, her laughter, her wisdom, and the way she makes me more of myself—if I could bottle up all those into a sermon, I'd have no need to write again.

My teachers lurk in the shadows of these pages, and I am profoundly grateful for their presence here and in the larger story of my life and learning. Some you will recognize by their influence on these words, their names already well-known to you. There are many others, friends and family, whose work and witness are of inestimable value to the corners of the world they occupy. I am blessed to count myself among those who have traveled through those corners, and am a better writer and person for having made the passage.

A special thanks to Michael Wilt and all the rest at Cowley Publications for looking over a manuscript with the eyes of hope, a rare gift in the publishing industry. Most of the world seems to operate out of an attitude of scarcity these days, but Cowley consistently seems to make choices based on abundance. Whatever becomes of this endeavor, I am glad for having made new friends in Boston.

We lost two great saints this past summer, my grandmother Jane ("Grannie") and my adopted grandfather, H.G. ("Papa J"). In the midst of our sadness, we were also celebrating the arrival of my first son, Henry, who showed up just in time to be held and loved by his great-grandparents. This book is dedicated to the memory of lives lost, and the promise of life received. On my desk as I write this, there is a picture of Grannie holding Henry just weeks before her death. It has become something of an anchor for me, allowing me to hold fast to an unfathomable grace. In the power of life lost and gained, my love for the three of them has made me much more aware of the sacred weight of each moment, the gentle in-breaking of the holy into the mundane.

So that's the life that I hope is in here, the life I wish for you as you begin this journey.

Introduction

In the thirty-second chapter of Genesis, there is this wonderful moment on the banks of the Jabbok where Jacob stands alone. Behind him is a life riddled with mistakes and miscalculations. By dressing up in cheap fur and a dash of his brother's cologne, he managed somehow to convince his blind father that he was actually Esau, the eldest son. In fooling his dad, he made off with the family blessing that was designated for Esau, but destined, somehow, for Jacob. But it does not feel like a blessing, it feels like a curse.

So now he stands on the bank of the river, which serves as sort of a temporary barrier to the inevitable catastrophe he has made of his life. Jacob conned Esau out of his birthright with a well-timed bowl of chicken soup, and, once Esau's hunger was abated, it was replaced by rage. Across the water waits Esau, and what Jacob imagines must be an insatiable urge for revenge and recompense. Staring at his shifting reflection in the water below, Jacob sees a desperate man. He has done everything he knows to do in such a situation, even praying. He has tried to run, but fast escapes are not really possible with eleven children and a herd of livestock. In an effort to fend off what he knows is coming, he has sent his brother gifts in apology; he has even sent his wives and children across the river in an attempt to soften Esau's anger. But now there is nothing, no one, left to send—but himself.

I come from that school of thought that recognizes there are perhaps no more poignant moments in life than the ones where we are broken beyond repair. The prophets and the desert monastics tried to simulate the desperation of life unraveled by denying themselves any creature comfort—trying to bring hair shirts back into fashion, snacking on bugs, if anything at all—thinking that the more empty spaces in their lives, the more space for God to inhabit. Perhaps they got the idea from reading this story, because there in the deep darkness, Jacob meets God.

Most of us spend our entire lives hoping for such an encounter. We envision our questions being answered, our hopes transformed into realities, every hole in our heart mysteriously filled. We don't have any clue as to what Jacob was expecting, but I'm willing to bet that this was not it. It is not a warm and fuzzy moment. There are no beautiful canticles, singing angels, or bright epiphanies. In fact, it looks more like a pay-per-view kickboxing championship than an encounter with the Holy of Holies.

Jacob finds himself in a face-off with God, though this meeting does not resemble any of the Sunday-morning niceties to which you may be accustomed. When Jacob meets God, it is a wrestling match. A battle. Neither side is willing to give up, so for hours they remain locked together in stubborn combat there by the riverside. It is a great struggle that lasts the entire night and leaves both combatants bruised yet strangely better off for their wounds.

Most of us have been so pre-conditioned by our faith communities that it seems strange to speak of faith and anger in the same breath. Rarely do we advocate contending with God. But one wonders if the anger that propels both sides to fight is not just a thinly veiled adoration, a radically compelling love that drives them to clash. Jacob, broken by his own faltering efforts, and God, love beyond measure, broken by nature. Maybe it's not so much a fight *against* the other as it is a fight to *hold on* to the other. Either way, as the sun rises, Jacob is left with a limp and a blessing. He names the place *Peniel*—the "face of God."

This book traces two stories—God's and our own—hoping that at more times than not, they will intersect. The first is told by the Christian calendar, the various seasons that structure our time as people of faith. The lectionary helps us to hear God's story in the chaos and confusion of our own. The amazing and frightening thing about it all is that when we begin to let ourselves be formed simply by the hearing of those words, by the telling of those stories, God's story starts to be told through the events of our own lives. In the blah-ness and the profundity of life, our days become living scripture.

I think of the lectionary calendar as an unpredictable tour guide. You sign up for the cruise to the Bahamas, but find yourself instead on the walking tour of Tehran. There is no telling where it will take you, but in handing ourselves over to its intentional reck-lessness, we will discover that faith is not just a matter of some moments, but the ground of all moments. The wisdom of the lec-tionary is that it incorporates the full range of human emotion, and calls it faith. There is doubt, fear, joy, triumph, wonder, pain, and all the rest somewhere in there. God is with us, Emmanuel, whether we can always see it or not.

There may be seasons that make more sense to you right now, so you may want to start there. If you're reading this book in the middle of spring, it may feel a bit silly to stand by the manger of Christmas. But this is not so much a seasonal devotional book as it is a witness to the seasons that cycle within our faith life. My hunch is that the better we understand the cycles of the story, the better we will understand the story itself and our place in it, the better we will be more fully at home in our skin.

Most of the chapters begin with a reading from the Bible, so that you'll have some sense of the original script before you hear my take on it. It might be helpful to have the Bible next to you while you read, in case you want to hear more of the story. There's certainly no need to know the Bible in order to read this book—in fact, those of you who haven't heard it all before are probably best prepared for hearing what the gospel really says. Those of us who have been around awhile have managed to chip away the rough edges, at least enough to make it presentable on Sunday morning. I'm also of the opinion that the Bible was always meant to be shared as a story, in community. To read it, to take it seriously, is to risk becoming a part of something larger than yourself. In the interest of full disclosure, I thought I should warn you: like Jacob, you're playing with fire.

There is nothing left to send over, nothing left to give, but our-selves. So here, on the edge of the Jabbok, uncertainty crouching on all sides, our heart broken and our hip out of place, let us tell the story one more time. Let us wrestle with the Teller, in hopes that we too, like Jacob, will receive our blessing. And may we all be granted hearts to know when the wrestling *is* the blessing.

Advent/Christmas: Waiting

We go forth
 into the cold and the darkness
 searching the skies, hungering for change, preparing for the
 unexpected.
Trusting that somewhere in the darkness,
 a light still burns
That in the dryness of the desert,
 a tiny branch still thrives
That in the most broken of human hearts,
 hope takes shape
That in a world bent on its own destruction,
 somewhere a child stirs in the womb.
May we be granted hearts to receive, eyes to see, and boldness to seek
 the birth of love into the world.
We go forth to prepare the way of the Lord . . .

I remember trying to learn the constellations in grade school. I remember it because I could never learn them. To this day, I have no idea how they got a crab, a scorpion, and Orion out of three or four dots in the sky. But I appreciate the imagination, to look up into the sky and see something more than chaos. Most of our days are spent staring at bits and pieces of God, wondering what to make of them. To see something in those seemingly random fragments is the work of faith. To trace a character, a self, out of the footprints of grace.

The Christian year begins in waiting. In the northern latitudes, at least, it is born out of cold bleakness. For those of us who don't live anywhere near the desert, it is the closest thing to it we may ever experience, a world that seems so empty of life that it's easy to forget there ever was such a thing as green. The target demographic for the season of Advent includes shepherds; unwed teenage mothers; and camel-riding, drop-everything-to-follow-an-extra-star-in-the-sky-that-nobody-else-happens-to-see "wise men." Like me, you may not easily place yourself within any of these groups, but in no way does that suggest that this time is not for you. Underneath their nativity-scene costumes, the thing that qualifies them for participation is not their station in life, but their lack of it. The mystery of Advent is that those to whom the world is blind will be the only ones with eyes to see the miracle that stirs in the straw. God has a sense of humor.

It is, among other things, the season of choice. It is when we decide whether we will believe in the things that are easy to swallow, or let ourselves be swallowed by the audacity of belief. Advent life is an existence that sees the world as it could be, but never with the rose-colored glasses of an empty optimism that selectively lets in only what it wants to. Instead, Advent inhabits the darkest corners of life, reinterpreting pathetic little branches on dead stumps as signs of a great victory. It crowns a child—born into poverty and the company of cattle, destined to end his life as sadly as it began—as a king. Advent invites us to take the broken pieces of our lives and world, and build a manger.

It is either madness or brilliance, or maybe even a bit of each. Either way, perhaps it's better to have risked the one for the other, than to have spent a life afraid of both. To risk believing that the random moments of meaning aren't so random after all, and that if we trace the shadows with our imaginations, we might just see the face of God.

2 The Theological Implications of Climate Control

O that you would tear open the heavens and come down, so that the mountains would quake at your presence—as when fire kindles brushwood and the fire causes water to boil—to make your name known to your adversaries, so that the nations might tremble at your presence! When you did awesome deeds that we did not expect, you came down, the mountains quaked at your presence. From ages past no one has heard, no ear has perceived, no eye has seen any God besides you, who works for those who wait for him. (Isaiah 64:1–4)

"And what I say to you I say to all: Keep awake." (Mark 13:37)

Sometimes without even realizing it, most folks think of life as a sort of progressive ladder. One event builds on another, and we move up one more rung to the next event that leads to something else and on and on and on. I think it's the lingering effects of those timelines we had to make in sixth-grade history. Somewhere along the line, we got the idea that this is the way the world works.

But nothing in nature—nothing really *alive*—ever works like that, and so it's a bit strange that we would expect the life inside us to conform to such artificial patterns. But instead of using natural

3

metaphors to understand our growth and development—like the seasons, or planets, or tides—we use technological thinking to understand ourselves, as if we are computers that can constantly be upgraded, headed down a one-way alley of growth, never to walk the same path twice. Forward, forward, forward.

I blame it on air-conditioning. Ever since we invented central heat and air, most of us live in the same temperature all year long. We are outside long enough to notice that the temperature is too hot or too cold, but then we're back inside where it's a comfortable 68.5 degrees, or whichever temperature you prefer, since we can adjust it to our liking. Nature has no power over us. We watch the five-day forecast on the news, to see what's coming next. My wife dabbled in marketing for a while, and was amazed to find that there is a great demand for CDs of the Weather Channel music. This is especially true of older folks, who evidently think that being able to leave the television locked on the weather all day long is a wonderful marvel of the modern age. My guess is that the music itself, albeit a charming mix of elevator/supermarket Muzak, is not the real attraction. The real draw is being able to avoid whatever nasties Mother Nature might try to throw our way. The airy, monotonous jazz, even without any lyrics, says in a bold voice, "We know what's coming."

That would not make much sense to our mothers and fathers in the Christian faith, whose insides were so profoundly shaped by what was going on outside that they saw their very being—life and faith and livelihood—all wrapped up in the cycle of the seasons. To drown out the voice of the world, to stop listening to what the winds and the rain and the sun are telling you, is to shut out the voice of God. Our ancestors in faith saw themselves not so much as passengers on a straight-line train, but as spokes in a common wheel, cycling through the same things every few months. It's not that they were living in a cosmic re-run, but that they understood the depth and wisdom that comes with returning to familiar places. This is a far cry from our modern sensibilities, which tell us that learning can only come from progress, newness, and innovation.

But despite our climate-controlled environments, our faith does not come with an adjustable thermostat. Our souls have not learned anything new in the past three thousand or so years. Our inner clocks are still set by the moon, our hearts still wander in circles, our ears are still holding out for that still small voice, no matter how much we want to fool ourselves into thinking that we are building some ladder to the person we want to end up being. The problem with that model is that you can always convince yourself you're not that person yet, and put off living your life one more day.

The truth is that the weather outside says much about the weather inside. The changes that bend and break nature are a promise that we too are meant for lives of dynamism and transformation. None of us is called to set up camp with one set of feelings or beliefs. We are not permanent residents in the town of religion: we are pilgrims on the journey of faith, and that means we are called to feel and think all different kinds of things at all different kinds of times. And fortunately or unfortunately, when God is leading you through the wilderness, there are more days than not that you swear you've been here before; you recognize your own footprint in the sand, and you realize you've made a huge circle of things. But there is a kind of growth that can only happen in cycles. To be alive is to welcome change.

There is perhaps no spot on the calendar where that is more obvious than in the days before Christmas. In these days of preparation, we are confused as to what to do with ourselves. The distorted supermarket Muzak (which you may recognize from the Weather Channel) insists that it is the "most wonderful time of the year," as if to say, "If you don't think so, there's something wrong with you." It seems surprising that so many people become depressed around Christmas, and we wonder how anybody could be sad during such a time. In the neighborhood where I live, there are enough plastic, light-up nativities to safely land a helicopter. There are awkward office Christmas parties. Santa Claus is in the mall, holding writhing children still for a keepsake picture. What's not to love?

But our bright lights and our merry songs don't really cover up the fact that the entire earth is depressed at this time of year. The leaves wither, the ground turns soggy and brown, the colors brighten only to disappear, the hours get shorter and the night gains strength, and there is no Christmas tree bright enough to swallow the darkness, no song loud enough to quell the silence. The weather is trying to tell us something.

Advent is about a lot of things we don't like very much. Waiting. Darkness. Change. Advent is the season that reminds us no matter how deeply rooted we think we are, no matter how firmly our feet are planted on the ground, no matter how sheltered we are from life's ups and downs, change is brewing. Not the kind of change you plan for. Not the kind of change you mark on your calendar. It's not the kind of change that fits easily into twelve steps. Advent change is the kind that comes all of a sudden, pulling the carpet out from under you, exploding in your ear. It comes in the darkness, in the cold, in the broken places. It respects nothing. It comes out of nowhere. It is devastating and fearful and beautiful and creative all at the same time. And it makes people do strange things.

Some would rather ignore it and get on with Christmas, which seems simpler for some reason. The cuteness of babies and manger animals versus the blackness of an empty sky, with no star of promise, no guiding light. So while the darkness rages on inside and out, we hang mistletoe, we fret over gifts and budgets rather than the tougher work of straightening out our own fears. We set plastic nativity scenes out on the front lawn. When God's light seems too dim, we call on the power company to oblige us. They are far more reliable, and they only demand our wallets, not our hearts.

Some of us get swallowed by the darkness. We can understand where Isaiah is coming from when he demands that God rip open the sky and do something for God's sake—*act like God for once.* Isaiah speaks for all of us when he yells up at the sky that we have had enough of not seeing, we have had enough of not hearing, we have had enough of this cosmic game of hide-and-seek. We have become like these dying leaves, bright for a while, but we are losing our grip and we will disappear into the ground all over again unless you do something. We are tired of listening to those tired, distorted choruses that God will be faithful, that God will show up, that God will make good on all these promises. We are afraid, and it is so much easier to give in to the fear—it seems so much stronger. Nothing is coming. Nothing is changing.

Then there are the rest of us who manage, through no ability of our own, to find our way through this confusing maze. We don't know where we're going, but somehow admitting that helps us get there. We don't know who we are all the time, but somehow knowing that makes us feel a little bit more at home in our lost-ness. And we don't have a quick or easy answer to wipe away the darkness and the frustration and the fear, but somehow not running from it makes it seem less powerful.

I don't want to take away from your Christmas. If your heart needs to move on, go with my blessing. But for the rest of you, those who are not quite sure about all this, I invite you to linger a bit longer in the shadows. In the uncertainty. In the darkness. Trusting that if we are patient enough to give ourselves over to Advent, wading through its murky unsteadiness, we will find some solid ground ahead. Trusting that if we will keep our eyes open to the darkness that wraps around us, resisting the urge to hurry up and light the rest of the Advent wreath, we will see the light of a new star—the light of God. Trusting that if we remain for a moment in the quiet, and keep ourselves from filling the silence with our own song, we will hear the trumpets of angels announcing the birth of love into the world. Trusting that if we hold off on the preparation for just a bit, living by the wisdom of God's creation rather than the pressure of our daily planners, we might find ourselves a bit better prepared for the surprise that is coming.

Let's stay out in the cold and the dark just a while longer...

3 The Loudest Silence

In the beginning when God created the heavens and the earth, the earth was a formless void and darkness covered the face of the deep, while a wind from God swept over the face of the waters . . . (Genesis 1:1–2)

There is perhaps no more hotly debated piece of scripture from the Hebrew Bible than this Creation story, which seems a bit strange. Everyone wants to find something different in there. Some read it as a biology textbook, therefore making it somewhat easier to pass judgment on. After all, biology textbooks are either correct or not worth the paper they're printed on. There's no place for poetry or hopefulness or human frailty, just right or wrong. The folks who approach the Bible this way tend to set themselves up in two vehemently opposed groups, with little room for discussion of the tougher questions posed by the scriptures themselves.

Other people want to read it with the eyes of history, finding themselves similarly polarized by what they find. In college, I attended a small church on the outskirts of town one Sunday, where the pastor spent the better part of an hour trying to convince his congregation that dinosaur bones were created by the government to discredit the Creation story. I'm not sure if any of my fellow worshipers were so persuaded, but the point he was arguing hinted at a much deeper human need: to know, with some degree of certainty, that God has something to do with us.

It should tell us something about the living witness of scripture that after several thousand years with the same story, we can't agree on what it says. It's certainly bigger than the words.

My own bias is that regardless of what you think about Darwin or God's creative powers, to reduce the Creation story to either a timeline or a cultural myth is to miss its power altogether. The Creation story is a love letter. It addresses the "whys" and "whos" of existence much more than it tackles the "whats" and "hows." To say that God created everything out of nothing is also a way of saying that the only thing that stands between us and nothingness is God. It speaks of God's fundamental nature, explaining God's need for companionship as it explains our own. It answers questions we didn't know we had—questions much too big for history or biology class to handle.

For those of us living in Advent time, it also traces out the path of new life. Its countercultural claim is that life begins out of nothing, out of darkness, *out of silence.*

It is the silence of awkwardness, where our truest selves seem to be laid bare and barren to the world. It is the silence that yearns to be broken by anything and everything, the silence that comes as punishment rather than relief. But it is also the silence that gives rise to our better selves, the quiet that brings with it listening and hearing, hurting and healing.

It is the rhythm of our own breathing. The stillness that helps us to hear that strange muscle hidden beneath our ribs, keeping us alive but also keeping us in a kind of death. The silence that holds out our deepest questions, the ones we mute with distractions, only to find them patiently waiting for these gentler times to wake us from our slumber. This is the silence of beginning, the silence of things new and old, beckoning us into wonder. This is where things begin.

It is here that we are reminded that the curtain between beauty and sadness is thin. It is here that we know, in that knowledge beyond words, that to know either joy or pain is to know both, which might explain why so many artists are the victims of their own creations, suffocated by a perspective that is theirs alone, citizens of a world that is at the same time a manipulative fiction and the truest of all truths. They spend their days birthing colors and insight and characters, only to find their creativity is a tragic sort of insanity, a seeing of things unseen. It is perhaps the most solitary loneliness to be creative, to peer so deeply into the human condition that the casual spectator experiences release, but the author can never disassociate from what she has seen. The ghosts that invited us into the story do not leave once the final page is written, the colors haunting the back of our eyelids long after the final stroke hits the canvas.

The story goes that God's breath swept across the waters, and that something in the chemistry of that moment created life. To be alive, to breathe, is to create more life. It is hard to say that God was not alive before creation, but it is certainly difficult to imagine the God that holds in Its breath. Asking such a being to refrain from creation is to ask it to stop being altogether. One imagines that God's lungs would burst from uselessness. Giving life is God's life, as much as our lives are built on the regular exchange of inhaling and exhaling. Creation is as much God's beginning as it is ours, God's self-discovery sprawled out into canyons and stars and daffodils.

There are no one-way streets here, no simple answers. Creation seems to blur our understanding of power, leaving all of us simultaneously puppets and kings. When we begin in such a place, our reason can take us great distances, sometimes farther than we ever expected, but it always ends with what we know. Our rational thinking can only shine light on that which is already ready to be seen; the darkest depths, the richest treasures, the questions not meant for answers—reason cannot take us there. It seems that there is a firm boundary between the sensible and the ineffable; both are great respecters of the other's border—reason stopping at the shore, wonder lurking in the depths of the inky black beyond.

So as we stand on the beach of imagination, our feet sloshed by the chill of the tide, our flesh stung by the breeze, and our ears drenched with its roar, we know that everything must change, or nothing will. We know that if we are to proceed, we must leave behind our reason; it cannot take us any farther.

It is time for a choice. We can stay behind, where our imaginations will remain in their seatbelts, where our colors will not run outside the lines. Where everything has a name and a proper place. We convince ourselves that we are content to follow the rules, to expect only the expected—get a job, start a home and family— to keep our eyes here on the shore. On the solid ground, where things are safe and somewhat predictable. We must be reasonable, we must believe that the realest things are the things we can see and touch and understand—the things we can hold. The rest is for children's bedtime stories—not for us. It is not that we are overly cautious, though of course we are—but we cannot risk breaking our hearts again on some foolhardy chance that this time will be different. So many of us will choose to stay.

But some of us have no choice. We must go. Our feet were made to dance between the stars, our eyes to envision the passion of the heart rather than the demands of the mind. Our words have the power to create a world, not just describe this one. Those of us who take the risk of belief trust that our home is somewhere out there on the horizon—in the thin veil between the light and the dark that beckons us into nothing—the nothing that is, that must be, something after all. There is always a chance that this might be it, that elusive mystery that we cannot name or describe but we know we have been waiting for. So we take a step, then another.

The water is deeper now, up to our knees, then our waists, then our chin, and there is much inside us that tugs us backward. We have been wired to not believe, to exercise caution, to criticize and doubt and refute, and our minds scream with these wiser, practical voices. But we belong to the current now, tangled in the impossible. And as we drift deeper and deeper into this ocean of wonder, we can make out a place that cannot be real but must be real all the same. A place where we feed rather than fight each other. A place without shadow, without uncertainty, where each step is taken with purpose. A place where God is as near to us as our own breath. We remember that we began this life breathing underwater, nurtured by a love we did not choose.

Here at the start of all things, don't assume that the silence is a lack of life. It may just be a love letter, whispered in the wind.

4 Peace for the Meantime

"But about that day and hour no one knows, neither the angels of heaven, nor the Son, but only the Father. For as the days of Noah were, so will be the coming of the Son of Man. For as in those days before the flood they were eating and drinking, marrying and giving in marriage, until the day Noah entered the ark, and they knew nothing until the flood came and swept them all away, so too will be the coming of the Son of Man. Then two will be in the field; one will be taken and one will be left. Two women will be grinding meal together; one will be taken and one will be left. Keep awake therefore, for you do not know on what day your Lord is coming. But understand this: if the owner of the house had known in what part of the night the thief was coming, he would have stayed awake and would not have let his house be broken into. Therefore you also must be ready, for the Son of Man is coming at an unexpected hour." (Matthew 24:36–44)

Rush-hour traffic. Results from the blood test. 286 megahertz. A little while. Just a minute. The 1970s soundtrack while the operator puts you on hold. The release date of anything involving Harry Potter. Christmas Eve. Reading the only magazine your dentist subscribes to, again. And again. Pregnancy. The click-click-click

13

of the roller coaster as it climbs the last and greatest hill on the track.

No one is "good" at waiting. It is not a virtue, it is something to be avoided. A problem. A kink. The enemy of technology and progress. We have aerodynamically streamlined every edge of our lives so that we can cut out the "waiting." You can do anything instantly now—grits, international telephone calls, oil changes, photographs—you name it, we can do it faster. What took us hours or days or weeks just a few years ago we can now do in minutes. When we call people on the phone, we no longer ask "how are you," we ask "where are you," because we know it could be anywhere. We are impatient. We are a people of superhighways, cell phones, the Internet on computers that will fit in our laps, express checkouts, and microwaves. We want what we want, and we want it now. Shortcuts, higher speeds, fewer steps—just no waiting.

But there is no escaping from time. We are trapped in it. No accessory for your Palm Pilot will give you more hours in the day. No matter how complex or expensive our watches are, they can't hurry the passage of a single minute. And the waiting drives us crazy, sometimes hurts us deeply. Waiting for promises that never get fulfilled. Waiting for healing that never comes. Waiting for a day when we feel better about ourselves. Waiting for God—to do something or say anything—waiting for God to be God.

We know that something is coming. There was a promise, words spoken that pointed to something—*anything*—happening.

And there is joy in that expectation, as there should be. Waiting sometimes means hope. But more often than not, we wait on that rickety old bridge between hope and disappointment. There is a fear that there will be no one in the end to make good on all these wonderful promises. That our prayers and our hearts are poured out into deep wells of nothingness. That when we make it to the end of the yellow brick road, there will be no wizard, only an unimpressive light show. When the wrapping paper is strewn all over the living room floor, when the turkey has been eaten, when the relatives have gone back home, there will be only quiet. And we will be left, wondering what it was all about, wondering what it was that we were waiting for.

Because waiting changes everything. It forces us to see differently. To live differently. We live our lives as if they are pending great change, as if each breath is taken on the precipice of something very, very important. As if each moment is not an accident, but a hint of what is coming, what must be coming. When Jesus said "one will be left" and "one will be taken," he was not just talking about salvation. He was talking about where people put their hope and their trust. In the same breath, he reminds us that the people in Noah's day kept living their lives, right up until the flood came. Of course they did—what else could they do? They were tired of the waiting. Tired of the silence on the other end of the line. Carpe diem and all that. Make the most of this time.

The secret, of course, is that no moment is an island. We cannot live in just the now, or just the past, or just the future for that matter. We belong to all three, and they belong to us. And as we stand squarely in the season of beginning, a newborn's cries at our back and a cloud of uncertainty ahead, the best truth we can muster is that we don't really know anything but this: Love will be born here. In the fractured pieces of our lives, in the hectic pace of our days, love will be born. And we will ignore it or resist it and even kill it, and it will just come again and again until we get it. Until we are able to see past the shiny veneer of these fragile lives into the darkness of an animal stall, the darkness of expectation. Until we are able to make our way to the side of a manger, to see the face of what we could not have expected.

Advent is the promise that the wait is not over, but it is worth it. The waiting is who we are, really. Because even in the waiting, even in the shadows, God will be with us. Emmanuel. It will not come on our schedule, it will not come as brightly packaged as we might want. There will be uncertainty, and doubt and fear, but there will also be wonder and hope and expectation. Make no mistake. God will come, whether we are ready for it or not. God will come. May we all be granted peace for the meantime.

5) The Theology of Dizziness

The light shines in the darkness, and the darkness did not overcome it. There was a man sent from God, whose name was John. He came as a witness to testify to the light, so that all might believe through him. He himself was not the light, but he came to testify to the light. The true light, which enlightens everyone, was coming into the world. He was in the world, and the world came into being through him; yet the world did not know him. (John 1:5–10)

Advent is the season of things that cannot be easily seen. It is the season of things that are not yet finished, things that can't really be spoken or described or imagined. It is something like waiting at the train station for a space shuttle, or opening your mouth to speak and hearing a language you don't know.

You should know up front that my own sense of reality is dramatically skewed by the environment in which I live and minister, the anomaly known as Academia. On the campus where I work, the beginning of the Christian year always coincides with the end of the semester. And whereas we begin each school year with more than adequate pomp and circumstance—orientation, convocations with academic regalia, official prayers, book-buying (and the unofficial prayers that accompany *that* experience), the handing-down of syllabi, fraternity and sorority rush—we end the semester with, well, nothing. Other than exams, the only regular rituals involve the unusual behaviors of students in crisis. There is the occasional creation of unexpected community, when they stay up late and eat irregular meals and talk with people they've never seen before because they're the only ones left in the computer lab. They laugh at things that aren't funny, all the while running around in twenty-five-degree weather in pajama pants. They stare blankly at books, reading the same page over and over again, hoping that there's enough room left in the human brain to soak up just a few more words. But other than these sporadic patterns, there is no ritual, no goodbye, no dramatic dis-orientation to send them home.

And whether or not you're in college, or have ever been there, chances are you are familiar with that moment when life turns upside down. When the structure you took for granted turns out to be made of sand, not granite, and you find yourself grasping for anything that will hold your weight. It is something akin to that moment right after your uncle has grabbed your hands and spun you around forty times at warp speed. But this time it doesn't wear off. The nausea doesn't go away, the horizon never comes back in focus.

Maybe you find yourself in that moment even as you turn these pages. If so, I think that your exhaustion or sadness or blah-ness or panic is the perfect key to understanding what this is all about. When you are confused and totally turned around backwards, you are in good company. The Bible was written by people in deep spells of dizziness, and contrary to what we might think, they considered the dizziness part of their qualifications for writing such a radically hopeful and sacred text. The Disciples were not brilliant mathematicians or Nobel scientists. They didn't have much in common and had no theological training, and that may be exactly why Jesus chose them and not the priests or the Pharisees or the Sadducees or any of the rest to stand by his side when it really mattered. Jesus didn't want people around him who were so sure of themselves they weren't ready to find out who they really were. He didn't want to travel with people whose feet were too firmly planted on the ground. He wanted dizzy people. Confused people. People whose hands were so slippery that they would know better than to try and hold on to something not meant to be held. People whose hearts were vulnerable enough that they would know when they were not doing the holding at all, but instead finding themselves held by something much, much bigger than they knew or wanted to know.

And when it came time to send out the invitations for the birth of a new king—not just any king, but the king of kings, a life so important that even its death would become a symbol of hope for the whole world—God chose not to invite dignitaries or ambassadors or people who would know what to wear and the polite things to say. The first guests couldn't talk at all—they were just dirty, smelly farm animals. Not the clean fluffy kind they keep at the petting zoo—the kind that live in their own perpetual disaster of smell and flies. The first *human* guests were shepherds, men who spend their lives watching animals eat and walk. There were the "wise men," whose only claim to wisdom was packing up their camels to chase some star into a foreign country. And there was the obscure young couple, poor and uneducated, exhausted and far from home, spending their first night as parents in a barn, wrapped up in the beauty and pain and cries and tears of a birth that almost could not have come at a worse time. God looked over the guest list and declared it to be perfect: "These—the confused and the brokenhearted and the unlikely—these are the guests for the birth of my child, these are the witnesses to love's arrival on earth." Alleluia, indeed.

And this child—the one for whom stars hung in the sky and angels sang and wise men walked—speaks of blessing and suffering in the same breath. He makes ridiculous promises, and outlines a world that is both impossible and impractical. He seems to be wiser than most but fails to see what is going on around him—fails to see that poverty doesn't equal happiness, that the poor aren't blessed, that the meek are lucky to make it through the rest of the day, much less inherit the earth. It is foolishness, really. To think that weakness is more powerful than power. To believe that our hope lies not in strength, but in the most desperate moment history could imagine. To humbly live out justice and kindness, trusting that there is no need for cunning or manipulation or greed. It is too much to believe; the first step is just too great. So just as we hope in this one (all the signs are right), everything in us tells us that the message is wrong, or else too right for us to swallow.

But this one, he seems to know where we've been. He seems to have as hard a time as we do staying still. So here at the edge of something new, we take a step and then another, trying to unlearn all the things we thought impossible. The way will not be easy, nor will it always feel like we are on the right path. Sometimes it will be so cloudy we will think we have lost the trail altogether. But the One who has called us here calls us on, into the foolishness and folly and mystery that is God's grace for us.

So in the wee hours of sleepless nights, remember the many unseen saints that surround you. Remember their fumbling, their misunderstanding, their lack of qualifications, their confusion. And remember the God who called them, who calls you even now, who seems to value mystery over answers, fog over clarity, and love over reason. Because you may just find yourself, in the midst of your dizziness, being called to follow a stranger from Galilee, or make your way to the side of his cradle.

Advent is the season of things that cannot be easily seen. But it is also the season when those of us who are most uncertain, most doubtful, most unlikely, find ourselves chosen by God. Stay dizzy. Watch the sky. Try to get some sleep. You're going to need your energy for the journey ahead. God is on the way.

6 Epiphany: The Discovering God

Inside our skin
  the heartbeat of a stranger
  pulses with a life we cannot control.
We hear the rhythm, calling us down a new road
  calling us into the story yet unwritten
  speaking our names in an unknown tongue.
We hunger for answers.
We hunger for definition.
We hunger to be known.

This is the only path we can take, the path that leads to self.

The path that leads to God . . .

Epiphany begins with the arrival of the wise men, whose questionable credentials have already been addressed in this book. But their discovery of the Christ child, for whom they have no religious vocabulary to describe, sets the tone for what the child will discover in himself.

Admittedly, it seems odd that we should talk of Christ's discovering himself. He is, after all, the Prince of Peace, the Son of

21

God, the Savior and Redeemer of the World. So something tells us that he should be exempt from all the messiness of personal development. We secretly hope that he has crib notes, a script, that tells him exactly how this will all go down. Then the story loses some of its edginess.

But in setting out fundamental Christian doctrine, our forebears had the wisdom (or wit) to proclaim that Jesus of Nazareth was somehow fully God and fully human at the same time. Rather than frustrating themselves with the ridiculous paradox of that declaration, they understood that God could only be contained in words that didn't seem to contain much of anything. God is in the mystery, in the nonsense, in the wonder.

There is no process more human than self-discovery. And in the portraits we have of Christ's life, we see the model for wrestling with and accepting the call of God. It is not something that happens for him in one moment, in one dramatic scene of divine encounter. It is rather a lifetime of little choices and big moments, waking every morning to discover God anew in the mundane and the profound.

Faith without change is nonsense. The tension of Christ's identity is now ours to tend, even as we are called to tend to the paradox within ourselves.

7 The Baggage of Vacation Bible School

Then one of the seraphs flew to me, holding a live coal that had been taken from the altar with a pair of tongs. The seraph touched my mouth with it and said: "Now that this has touched your lips, your guilt has departed and your sin is blotted out." Then I heard the voice of the LORD saying, "Whom shall I send, and who will go for us?" And I said, "Here am I; send me!" (Isaiah 6:6–8)

Once while Jesus was standing beside the lake of Gennesaret, and the crowd was pressing in on him to hear the word of God, he saw two boats there at the shore of the lake; the fishermen had gone out of them and were washing their nets. He got into one of the boats, the one belonging to Simon, and asked him to put out a little way from the shore. Then he sat down and taught the crowds from the boat. When he had finished speaking, he said to Simon, "Put out into the deep water and let down your nets for a catch." Simon answered, "Master, we have worked all night long but have caught nothing. Yet if you say so, I will let down the nets." When they had done this, they caught so many fish that their nets were beginning to break. So they signaled their partners in the other boat to come and help them. And they came and filled both boats, so that they began to sink. But when Simon Peter saw it, he fell down at Jesus' knees, saying, "Go away from me, Lord, for I am a sinful man!"

> *For he and all who were with him were amazed at the catch of fish that they had taken; and so also were James and John, sons of Zebedee, who were partners with Simon. Then Jesus said to Simon, "Do not be afraid; from now on you will be catching people." When they had brought their boats to shore, they left everything and followed him. (Luke 5:1–11)*

The time of Epiphany in the Christian calendar is just what it sounds like—when you have an epiphany, there is a flash, an insight, some new understanding. Whereas in Advent we were all in the business of waiting, expecting, Epiphany is the declaration that the Christ has come—what we were waiting for has finally arrived. The scriptures that the church reads immediately following Christmas are all flashes of Christ's identity—moments when the people around Jesus and we as readers suddenly catch a glimpse into who this man really is, what he is about, why he has come. It is the season of Christ's self-discovery, just as it is the season of our discovering this stranger from Nazareth turning out to be none other than the Messiah. It is the season of signs, moments of clarity and discovery. Epiphanies.

And if we are honest with ourselves, that is usually how God comes to us in our daily lives. Most of us are just given brief moments of clarity, moments when things make sense about life and the world and God and anything else that is confusing us. We are always in some state of in-between-ness, waiting for something to toss us up or pull us down. Waiting for an epiphany.

These scriptures are exactly the kind of stories Vacation Bible School teachers love to teach—Isaiah's call in the temple comes complete with angels and seraphim and smoke and everything that makes for a good Steven Spielberg movie, and Simon Peter's call has fish. Every good Vacation Bible School story needs fish, because there is always a hefty supply of those goldfish-shaped crackers on hand. And it makes sense that we would want to tell these stories to children. They are amazing. God breaks into the world, speaking through the smoke and the fog. Jesus comes out of nowhere and calls two fishermen who are just minding their own business one minute, and the next they have left everything to follow him. These are beautiful, inspiring stories. The thing is, if you are anything like me, you end up with a lot of psychological baggage after hearing these stories over and over again in that context. There is always a part of me that longs to be singled out by God in the temple, spoken to directly by Jesus. There is a clarity—an epiphany—to these moments that seems so attractive.

Epiphany also coincides with Black History Month, a time for us to hear stories from the past and hopes for the future. But there is this part of me that hears stories, particularly from the civil rights era, stories about Martin Luther King Jr. and Rosa Parks, and I find myself having the same reaction I do with these biblical stories. It seems so clear to me when I watch a film or read the history of the 1950s and '60s—it seems so obvious what the issues were, what needed to be done. I find myself wishing to live in a different time, a time of passion, when the lines between good and evil seemed so clear. A time when God seemed to be much more evident in daily life, calling people into action, into courageous prophecy.

There is a deep desire in every human heart to hear our names spoken by God. To have a moment where our lives fall out before our eyes, where our path becomes illuminated, where our steps take on new purpose. Whatever our station in life, no matter our age, no matter how many years we have graced the pews at our local church, there is a secret, unspoken yearning to hear the sound of God's voice, even if we stopped admitting it a long time ago. To have a purpose and reason to be in the world.

But the silence remains, so we work especially hard at *making* a calling for ourselves. We decide what it is that we are good at, what we want to be when we grow up, what we like best. And that goes well for a while, but there is a gnawing uncertainty sometimes in the pit of our stomachs that says there must be more. We look around us and in that strange, deceptive way, our hearts tell us that we are alone in our uncertainty. Other folks around us seem much more sure of themselves, of who they are supposed to be. Their lives seem, from our view, filled with clarity and direction, while our own direction is more of an approximation we had to make because it was time to pick one and we had to do it. All of our decisions seem more like compromises rather than holy mandates. And for those of us who spend time around other Christians, it can be even worse, because then our lack of direction becomes a theological issue. We've all been around those folks who seem to have a straight shot to God's mouth, who have these burning bush experiences all the time and talk about every decision they make as "the will of God." As much as we want to facilitate our own vocation, our own calling, it doesn't ever seem to work the way we expect.

So most of us eventually give up. We don't call it that, but we finally decide on being something just so we can stop the chaos, stop the waiting. We jump into a job or a relationship so that we can get out of the stormy waters of indecision, so that the voices of our own questions will quiet down a little. So that we will have an answer for the family interrogators who surround us at Thanksgiving, wanting a quick and simple answer to what we're "doing with ourselves." Because somewhere along the line, we got sold the message that being mature and being a good Christian and a good person means certainty and stability. So that if you are uncertain or unstable, you are neither a good person nor a faithful one.

But when you read these Bible stories a little more closely, I don't think that's the message at all. Read the Isaiah story again, trying as best you can to ignore all the voices that told you what it's about. Read the part about where the angel puts a burning coal on his tongue, and decide for yourself whether or not *that*'s a pleasant experience. Pay attention to how he describes when this all happened, in the year of King Uzziah's death, a time of mourning and chaos. Like other folks called by God, Isaiah doesn't jump at the chance. In fact, he spends most of his energy here at the beginning of his ministry trying to convince God that he's not the right man for the job. And this feeling doesn't go away with time, for Isaiah is called on to deliver bad news over and over again to his people. God doesn't tend to enlist the services of prophets when things are going well—that "burning coal sensation" on his tongue is the first of many times it will break Isaiah's heart to speak God's word.

The same with Peter and the goldfish cracker story. Here's an incredibly normal guy living his life who is in the wrong place at the wrong time. And his call? It comes not in a convenient, prepackaged worship service, or with a detailed life plan. Instead it comes with him standing knee-deep in fish, on a boat that's about to sink, with someone he's just met. And Peter's life will not smooth out into a peaceful existence. It will be filled with mistakes, doubts, missed chances, the loss of his friends.

And as much as we want to romanticize the civil rights era, the issues were no clearer to those living in those times than the issues are for us today. For every hero with wisdom and insight and every villain determined to keep his neighbors living in oppression, there were two hundred normal folks who didn't know which way was up or down. And for every moment that a Martin Luther King Jr. or a Rosa Parks had clarity, for every moment of decisiveness that makes for a good story, there were a thousand moments of uncertainty in between.

There is nothing wrong with you if you're not sure what God wants of you. In fact, I'm of the opinion that it's up to you and God to work that out in your own time. And I hope that you get a moment when everything is clear, when you know how your life is supposed to play out, but that will certainly be different from my life and I'm pretty sure that's not the biblical model, either. The trick of living the Christian life is just to keep your bags packed, so that you're ready to respond whenever you find God showing up in your life—whether it's in a temple filled with smoke or in a sinking boat or in a bus in Montgomery on December 1, 1955. The difference between the folks who get called and those who don't is not merit or skill or how much God loves them; it's whether they're willing to wait in the uncertainty, in the normal moments, in the interims, for the brief and awkward moments of Epiphany.

God will call. Make no mistake. It may not sound the way you expect it to, it may not come when you're ready to hear it, but God will call. But, until then, our task is to wait—always holding out ridiculous hope, listening even when it hurts. For chances are, if you are feeling overwhelmed, directionless, feeling that there is no place for you in the world, you aren't alone at all, but standing in the presence of the One who has come to call you to life. And my prayer for you and for me is that when the call comes, we will have the stupidity and the naïveté to say yes in that same shaky voice that Peter and Isaiah and Martin and Rosa did. Yes, Lord, we will follow.

8 The Apron on the Floor

When he came to Nazareth, where he had been brought up, he went to the synagogue on the sabbath day, as was his custom. He stood up to read, and the scroll of the prophet Isaiah was given to him. He unrolled the scroll and found the place where it was written: "The Spirit of the Lord is upon me, because he has anointed me to bring good news to the poor. He has sent me to proclaim release to the captives and recovery of sight to the blind, to let the oppressed go free, to proclaim the year of the Lord's favor." And he rolled up the scroll, gave it back to the attendant, and sat down. The eyes of all in the synagogue were fixed on him. Then he began to say to them, "Today this scripture has been fulfilled in your hearing." All spoke well of him and were amazed at the gracious words that came from his mouth. They said, "Is not this Joseph's son?" (Luke 4:16–22)

There is a lot that is known about Jesus' life that is interesting, but the thing that fascinates me is the time we don't know. In particular, I want to know what happened during those missing years—that big jump the Gospels make from "when he was a cute little baby" to the time he was walking around telling stories about scattered seeds, houses built on sand, and all the rest. What I would most like to ask Jesus is what he was doing during all that time, whether he was thinking about what was coming or whether he was just enjoying life and then one day dropped his hammer and laid down his carpenter's apron.

I think if I could know what happened during that time, it might give me a clue as to where all his courage came from, or why he didn't start his ministry earlier, or what he really missed about his old life when he hit the road for the first and last time. What was he waiting for?

Maybe he knew that this was a one-way road. That he'd never be able to come back home. Maybe that's why he waited so long, thirty years, before he went out and did anything. Maybe he was afraid, or unsure of when he was supposed to get started, or how to start at all. I wonder what Mary and Joseph told him about the circumstances of his birth, or about the gold, frankincense, and myrrh that had been sitting on the fireplace mantel as long as he could remember. Did they have to tell him? Or did he just know? These are the things that I want to know because at some point in that time period, something changes in Jesus. He gets a calling, or maybe he just finally accepts his calling—whatever it was, he realizes one day that he belongs out there, not in the workshop, not at the table with his mother's cooking, not with his friends, but out there. Down the road.

And you might remember what happens after that—there's that rather frightening John the Baptist guy, who is into wearing dead animals and eating bugs with honey. We all stood there on the side of the river, watching Jesus get dunked by John, wondering why he even needed to be baptized, but especially why he needed to be baptized by such a scary, loud guy whose breath smelled like locusts. We were going to ask him at the reception afterwards, but he slipped out when we weren't looking and headed for the desert, of all places. And he must have been gone for at least forty days, doing who knows what out there, but he came back with a look in his eye. I can't really describe it, but maybe you've seen it yourself. It's like he suddenly knew where he was going, what was waiting for him, like he was staring at some landmark down the road none of the rest of us could see.

And he marches from the desert right into his old home church there in Nazareth, shaking the sand off his feet. And they thought it might be nice to let him give his first sermon. As someone who has gone back to his home church to give a sermon, let me tell you it can be a really awkward experience, and maybe you know what I mean.

The first stage of adulthood is humiliation, where people you have known for a while suddenly want to tell a lot of stories about your childhood. It's as if they have been holding out for all these years, and now they just can't help but tell every single thing they remember about you as a kid. There is an unspoken code of behavior for such people, which requires that every time they lay eyes on you the first thing out of their mouth is "I remember when you . . ." These type of people frequent local churches. There were several holidays in college when I avoided my home church altogether, because inevitably some strange woman whom I swear I had never seen before would walk right up to me, attempt to remove my cheeks with her knuckles, and tell me how she used to change my diaper. And evidently a lot of people used to change my diapers.

For Jesus, these are the "in-between" times—you are ready to make your way into the land of adulthood. But all these other people—the people who have known you the longest—keep trying to hold you back. They are struggling to figure out what to make of you. There is this rich history of diapers and things you said and things you broke that they want to hold onto because while it is of little value to you other than its potential for embarrassment, it is precious to them. It is a part of who you are. And so you are stuck "in between" who you have been and what you are becoming. And most of us would rather focus on the future or on what we are doing now, so we avoid those places where our pride and our cheeks may be in peril.

So when Jesus marches up to the front of the church and begins reading from Isaiah, everybody is ready to hear some nice simple sermon about how much the church has meant to him and "thanks for the kind notes of support while I was in the desert," but instead he just reads the scripture—*The spirit of the Lord is upon me, because he has anointed me to bring good news to the poor.* Not the best start, but certainly he'll recover. I suppose the poor need some good news. *He has sent me to proclaim release to the captives.* Now he's going to need to get approval for that; you can't just go around releasing captives. *And recovery of sight to the blind.* Well now that's nice, kind of a big goal, but that's nice. *To let the oppressed go free.* Alright, he's already released the captives; if we've got the captives and the oppressed running around . . . *To proclaim the acceptable year of the Lord.* And it's over. Well, maybe not.

Because as soon as he finishes speaking, he rolls up the scroll, hands it to the minister there at First Church Nazareth, and says something the gist of which is: "All that I just said, about a time for the captives and the oppressed and the good news for the poor, it just started." Now that would be hard for any crowd to swallow, but this isn't just any crowd. This crowd is those cheek-shaking, diaper-changing people that meet you when you go home. And they cannot believe what they see. One of them is even bold enough to shout out, "Where did he get all this?" "We know who you are—you're Mary and Joe's kid. You used to cut my grass. You can't be the Messiah." And then, Luke tells us, only moments after warmly welcoming him, the congregation comes frighteningly close to tossing him off a nearby cliff.

Not that I blame them. Who does he think he is, strutting in here and turning the whole world upside down? He's got to be mad. Doesn't he know his place? Has he even been paying attention?

So what happened to him in those in-between times, those times we know nothing about, to drive him to such extremes? Surely it was something dramatic, to end thirty years of quiet living for a brief stint flipping the world upside down.

Maybe he had just seen too much suffering. Maybe he lived, as we do, in a country where the fastest-growing homeless population is children under the age of 12. Maybe he knew already that in just one day, just today, an estimated 25,000 children would die from hunger and malnutrition. Maybe he was tired of how unfair things were, thinking about how Christians make up one-third of the population, while controlling two-thirds of all the wealth and spending 97 percent of it on themselves. Maybe he was angry at how Americans, many of whom would call on his name, would spend $17 billion a year on pet food, while according to the United

Nations Human Development Report it would only take an additional $11 billion a year to make sure that everyone in the world had basic food and healthcare. Maybe that's why he had to do it.

Maybe he was tired of hearing people say, "You can't change the world. There's no hope for that. Just settle down. Those are silly little dreams you're having. They'll go away as soon as you find a nice house out in the suburbs. Just calm down." Maybe he was tired of ignoring those voices inside his head that told him he *could* do something. That he *had* to do something.

Maybe it was one of those reasons. Maybe there are others that we can't even imagine. But here's my guess: he was looking for God. My guess is that he knew enough to know that if God was anywhere, he wasn't just in the pretty stained-glass windows of the temple or in the pages of his Bible. He knew that God was out *there*, in the suffering of God's people. That God was out there where the racism was, where the hunger was, where little kids were spending all day in sweatshops in Bangladesh so that American kids could buy cheap, trendy clothes. That God was out there wherever someone needed to be clothed or fed or taught or listened to or held or healed.

And the other thing I think Jesus knew was that God had made only one of him. That if he didn't listen to his heart, if he didn't find his place in the world, then no one else would do it for him. And once he did that, once he knew that he really had no other choice but to be himself, he had to leave that dusty old shop.

And for those of us who choose to spend any time around this fellow, there is also a choice. We can be the people others expect us to be. We can fall in line and live normal, quiet lives to ourselves. Or we can be naïve enough to be the people God created us to be, believing—even though it makes absolutely no sense—that we can change the world just by being who we are. Not by being Jesus, or Mother Teresa, or Martin Luther King—that was their job—but by being Brian and Heather and Luke and Jennifer. To drop our carpenter's aprons and our fears and our self-doubt to the floor. To walk out into that world and start living a revolution. You know the one I'm talking about. The one about the captives and the oppressed and the blind and all the rest.

It starts now.

9 The Answer We've Been Waiting For

As soon as they left the synagogue, they entered the house of Simon and Andrew, with James and John. Now Simon's mother-in-law was in bed with a fever, and they told him about her at once. He came and took her by the hand and lifted her up. Then the fever left her, and she began to serve them. That evening, at sundown, they brought to him all who were sick or possessed with demons. And the whole city was gathered around the door. And he cured many who were sick with various diseases, and cast out many demons; and he would not permit the demons to speak, because they knew him. In the morning, while it was still very dark, he got up and went out to a deserted place, and there he prayed. And Simon and his companions hunted for him. When they found him, they said to him, "Everyone is searching for you." He answered, "Let us go on to the neighboring towns, so that I may proclaim the message there also; for that is what I came out to do." And he went throughout Galilee, proclaiming the message in their synagogues and casting out demons. (Mark 1:29–39)

In the season of Advent, we read scriptures about God's promises, and I imagine that if you are like me, you tend to see what you need to see in God's promises. That is the beauty and wonder of expectation—when it is only in our heads, we can shape it to fit the holes in our own lives. If we are lonely, we imagine the richness of good company. If we are hungry for direction, we imagine a golden path popping out of nowhere to carry us to the one place we really belong. If we are hurt, we do our best to imagine some freedom from our suffering, some balm for our pain. And in the darkest times, it is our hope of the unknown, our belief that something could fill those empty spaces, that keeps us going.

But when expectation becomes reality, something changes. When your dreams pop out of your head and are suddenly standing there in front of you, well, it's a little disappointing.

Advent is about a dream. It is about expectation, about imagination. We line up with all our questions in tow, waiting for God to show up and make good on all these promises. And when that happens, we're all a bit confused. Epiphany is the reality of God's answer to our hopes. But it's not right, it doesn't fit. The answer—the answer that is supposed to be the answer of all answers, the thing that will wipe away every tear and solve every problem—well, it looks an awful lot like . . . *us*. It seems too fragile and unpredictable and unglossy to be God. It gets angry. It gets afraid. It cries. It doesn't just look like us, it *is* us. Human. No cape, no super powers, no batmobile, just another one of us. And we can't help but thinking, this isn't what we needed. This isn't what we asked for.

But there are always some that are so close to their desperation, so broken by the unfairness of life, that any answer seems like the right one. That is why the Bible is so filled with common people and peasants and untalented nobodies, rather than kings or scholars. The kings and scholars have already made up their mind what's best for them, and have fooled themselves into the awful assumption that they can take care of themselves. God seems to connect better with the powerless, the weak, the rejected, not because they are holier or secretly more deserving, but probably, I suspect, because they are the only ones who still recognize their need for God. They are the only ones left who don't have to argue about God's existence or the finer points of eschatological theology, because their need of God—their absolute dependence on God's love—tells them that God is indeed real.

So when Jesus heads into Galilee, to visit Simon's sick mother-in-law, word spreads like wildfire through the impoverished homes of that countryside. Maybe if Jesus had been around the more well-to-do subdivisions, he would have been left alone. Those folks know how to behave, or at least how to keep to themselves. But here, huddled with his friends in a tiny home, he is discovered for what he is—the answer. And so as he peers out the window at the countless hundreds of ill and wounded and broken people that press in on the house, he is overwhelmed by the sheer hurting. He heals so many, but there are so many more. It seems that for every person he touches there are ten new ones standing in line. And after hours and hours of facing the darkness, he is exhausted. He hardly sleeps that night—he is far too tired—and as soon as he can, he slips out of the house to find a quiet spot to be alone. To pray, to reconnect. To remember what all this is for.

The disciples find him there, looking as if he has just run a marathon or been in a wrestling match or worse. "Everyone is looking for you," one of them finally whispers. "What should we tell them?" And there, after hours of prayer and days of exhaustion, Jesus stands at a turning point. Centuries later, Martin Luther King Jr. would find himself in the same place, making the same decision, sitting at his kitchen table, staring blankly at a cup of coffee. Martin desperately wanted out of the whole thing. He was afraid. His family had been threatened. The window panes in his home bore the evidence of gunshots, and only three days later half of his home would explode from a terrorist's bomb. The thousands of African Americans in Montgomery and soon throughout the country were beginning to see him as their answer, and that pressure was crushing him. The task was too great, the burden too heavy, the road too long. He was too young. He had his own church to tend to, and most importantly, he didn't believe he had it in him to be this person. *The answer.*

And in that moment, sitting in the quiet of his kitchen, Martin had his first real experience of God. And he realized that it was not his road to walk by himself, not his burden to carry alone, but that there was a God, a God who believed in justice, and would never leave his side. And that assurance gave him the strength to go forward.

Jesus looked at his disciples, remembering the people who were waiting for him at Simon's house, thinking of all the people in the other villages, pulled between all the places that needed him, all the brokenness and pain—*there were so many others* . . . "It is time to go," he told his friends. "There are others who need to hear this message." And with that, the group set off, into the uncertainty of a path that only their leader could know.

There comes a time when we all must face the dueling voices of the world's pain and our own inability to make a difference. When we have to decide whether injustice is simply a part of life, or the enemy of it. A time when we have to choose what voices we will hear—the voices that speak of our own frailty, that wish for an answer to drop from the sky, the voices that tell us if only this were different, we would act. Or the voice that says, "I am with you. I am always with you, and that will be enough."

When we gather around the common table, Christ's table, we remember that it is the promise of God's kingdom on earth, where everyone has a place, everyone has a voice, everyone has justice. Where all of us, regardless of our differences, find a seat at the same table. For we are not in charge of the invitation list, only the inviting. That is the frustrating beauty of grace. The only thing more difficult than earning God's love is trying to lose it. And so as we accept our invitation to the feast, let us take note with heavy hearts those of our brothers and sisters who are not with us. May the wine burn in our throats, giving us the courage to speak for them. May the bread give us the energy to act for them. May the table be our turning point, and may we find that somewhere, deep in our hearts, the answer we've been waiting for is us.

10 Hearing the Same Old Thing for the First Time

Nicodemus said to him, "How can these things be?" Jesus answered him, "Are you a teacher of Israel, and yet you do not understand these things? Very truly, I tell you, we speak of what we know and testify to what we have seen; yet you do not receive our testimony. If I have told you about earthly things and you do not believe, how can you believe if I tell you about heavenly things? No one has ascended into heaven except the one who descended from heaven, the Son of Man. And just as Moses lifted up the serpent in the wilderness, so must the Son of Man be lifted up, that whoever believes in him may have eternal life. For God so loved the world that he gave his only Son, so that everyone who believes in him may not perish but may have eternal life. Indeed, God did not send the Son into the world to condemn the world, but in order that the world might be saved through him." (John 3:9–17)

For whatever reason, some scriptures speak louder than others. They jump out off the page at you, as if they were written by someone who knows you as well as you know yourself. It's somewhat similar to finding a message in a bottle, that you know in your head was written for anyone, but your heart whispers of the many hidden reasons that you alone have come to read it.

39

And of those scriptures, the ones that make us think more or make us feel as if the Bible may have been written just for us, there is perhaps none more famous than this passage from the third chapter of John. We wave it at baseball games, have it emblazoned on our coffee mugs, stick it to the bumper of our car, because it seems to say everything that needs to be said in just a handful of words—twenty-seven in the New Revised Standard Version, twenty-five if you're reading the Greek—only a drop out of the Bible's ocean, but a drop that carries a message that feels like it is for us.

Of course, the one it was originally intended for was named Nicodemus. A good man, by all accounts, a Pharisee's Pharisee, who had spent his life doing his best to measure up. Maybe you know the type: elected class president of the Pharisees (class of '05), first-born and pride of his parents, named to the *Who's Who in Pharisees Today* list more times than you could count, always in the right place doing the right thing.

In fact, Nicodemus was so good at being good, you might think to look at him that he had it all figured out. That he knew what he wanted from life and what all this was for. That's, at least, how everyone had always treated him, so he had spent his life taking care of other people's problems, listening to their questions and doubts, reassuring them when they were uncertain, shaking hands and doing very well for himself.

But like many of us, Nicodemus carried around a secret. Not like a secret password, or the location of a treasure or anything like that. In fact, if you asked him to tell you what his secret was he probably wouldn't know what you're talking about. But beneath the shiny veneer of Nicodemus's extraordinary faith and life, beneath that person who colored in the lines so well, who seemed to never make any mistakes, was a man who was living on a steady diet of nothing.

He could say the right answers, but he never got to ask the questions. He could care for others in their moments of deep doubt and pain, but he was afraid to ever go near the broken places in his own heart. Instead of really receiving love, instead of hearing any of those compliments people were always throwing his way, Nicodemus kept trying to make himself feel better by becoming better—by studying more, pleasing more people, working harder, as if the more energy he spent the better he might feel about himself. But maybe you have tried that equation before, the one where you try to receive love by earning it, and you know how badly that works. It's like quicksand; the more you try, the deeper you sink.

So one cool summer night, when he cannot ignore the hole inside him anymore, he sneaks off to find a teacher by the name of Jesus, who seems to have it all together. Who seems to have figured it out. Who might just have the answer to what Nicodemus needs.

But if you've read the story before, maybe you know that Nick was asking for something Jesus wasn't giving. Nicodemus was looking for what he needed to do in order to feel better—give to the poor? Pray more often? Spend more time in church? Memorize scripture? What was it? And if you've ever been in Nicodemus's shoes, so desperate for an answer, you know that you're basically willing to do anything that you're told—you'll try anything that might fill that hole.

But when Jesus' answer comes, it sounds more like a question. "You must be born from above—born again—if you want to feel better," says Jesus. And just to show how desperate Nicodemus really is, for a moment, he takes this advice literally. *You want me to crawl back up into the womb? That's what I need to do? But how? I can't . . .*

What Nicodemus wants is a way to make himself feel worthy. It is perhaps the most basic religious instinct in any of us, to want to feel like we belong in our own skin, to calm the restless voices inside us that tell us we are not enough, we don't do enough, we don't have enough. In a lot of ways, he's not much different from Isaiah or Moses or Peter or Ruth or any of the rest of those folks in the Bible who came in contact with God—our immediate reaction is always our lack, our unworthiness, that God must have the wrong number. Of all God's miraculous acts, it is God's choosing us that is the hardest to believe.

And as Nicodemus sits there, pondering the biological impossibility that has just been laid at his feet, he misses the door that has just been opened in front of him. Because what Jesus is really saying, in his typical easier-than-it-sounds vernacular, is that we all need a do-over. We need to recognize that there is nothing we can

41

do to earn or lose God's love, so as long as we are searching for that one thing, we will be searchers only, never finders. If there were something that any of us could do to deserve God's love, there would have to be some way to lose it, too, and that doesn't seem to be the kind of world God is interested in.

It's as if Jesus is saying, "If you want to know that God loves you, stop trying to make God love you and open your eyes—because here, in this flesh and bone, in my teachings and my death and my life again—here is the promise that God loves you just as you are." So maybe it is good that we keep waving our signs around, keep wearing this promise on our T-shirts and baseball caps, if we think that will convince anybody, including ourselves, that God loves us. It's the most oft-repeated phrase within the walls of the church, but it is the one to which the walls of our hearts are most impermeable.

I have nothing to convince you otherwise, just a handful of words. And this invitation: to believe for just a moment that you were created out of love, that God is already embracing you, already accepting you. The difference between the really happy people and the otherwise is just that some are willing to wake up one morning, though everything looks the same, and believe that they get a new start. A do-over. Not a second chance—that would imply that the pressure is even greater to get it right. No, this is an invitation to participate in the creation of a new world, starting inside each one of us, where people get to screw up, get to be honest about their shortcomings, and get to unwrap that gift that has been gathering dust on the front step—unconditional love from an unconventional God.

11 The Unauthorized Autobiography

He came down with them and stood on a level place, with a great crowd of his disciples and a great multitude of people from all Judea, Jerusalem, and the coast of Tyre and Sidon. They had come to hear him and to be healed of their diseases; and those who were troubled with unclean spirits were cured. And all in the crowd were trying to touch him, for power came out from him and healed all of them. Then he looked up at his disciples and said: "Blessed are you who are poor, for yours is the kingdom of God. Blessed are you who are hungry now, for you will be filled. Blessed are you who weep now, for you will laugh. Blessed are you when people hate you, and when they exclude you, revile you, and defame you on account of the Son of Man. Rejoice in that day and leap for joy, for surely your reward is great in heaven; for that is what their ancestors did to the prophets. But woe to you who are rich, for you have received your consolation. Woe to you who are full now, for you will be hungry. Woe to you who are laughing now, for you will mourn and weep. Woe to you when all speak well of you, for that is what their ancestors did to the false prophets." (Luke 6:17–26)

There are moments in the Gospels when the storyteller seems to remember the details a little differently from the way the others do. For example, Luke has shepherds come to the birth of baby Jesus, Matthew invites the wise men, John spends his first chapter relating the birth of Christ to the beginning of time itself, and Mark just starts his story with a 30-year-old man. They all remember Christ saying different things from the cross, but they put things in different order. Jesus doesn't tell any parables in the Gospel of John, but he performs some miracles the others don't mention, including being able to knock over some armed guards just by saying the words: "That's me."

And depending on how you look at it, it can be very frustrating to have four different versions of the same story. It's even more overwhelming when you start to read all the other Gospels that didn't make it into the Bible. Most people, when they realize that the Bible doesn't work like a science book, just want to give up on it. It must not be true, if these stories don't all agree in every detail. I tend to think that it must be *truer* than anything else in print, because when you think about it, the moments that mean the most to us, the ones that shape who we are and what we're about—we tend to remember those moments in our own way. We pick up on words and smells and sights that others don't, because they're the ones that speak to us. Ask a family of four kids to talk about the vacation they just took together with their parents, and you will get four very different stories, all true, all full of meaning and memory and love. Sometimes it's as if the story itself has a life of its own, that the hearts of the story and its teller are one and the same. It's something akin to having four camera angles, all seeing Jesus' life and ministry and life again from a different perspective, all seeing the same thing, but seeing it through four sets of lenses, four stories, four different hearts.

For now, Luke is our camera. You have heard this story before, probably called the "Sermon on the Mount," because Matthew tells us it happened on top of a mountain, where Jesus went to teach his disciples. Luke, however, finds Jesus standing in a level place, somewhere on the plain. It is still the early stages of his ministry, and after walking from town to town, having strangers join him and then disappear again, Jesus has finally figured out which seem to be the ones who have nowhere else to go. The ones who are staying with him for the whole journey. He goes off by himself

THE UNAUTHORIZED AUTOBIOGRAPHY

for the night, prays for guidance, just as he does with every major decision in the Gospel of Luke, and the next morning, calls them. The twelve. From all the crowds of folks who follow him, who listen to what he says, he finds twelve rough and ragged friends to stand by him. To follow in his steps and share his path.

And there as they stand on that flat piece of ground, not knowing whether this is an honor or a curse they have just received, the twelve are joined by a crowd again. People from all over the place—Tyre and Capernaum, Chattanooga and El Paso—are all crowding in on him. People with broken bones and infections, people with fevers and leprosy, people with broken spirits and broken hearts. And as they move in on each other, trying to catch a glimpse of Jesus, trying to jockey their way through the crowd to be right next to him, to have the best seat for the healing and teaching, they each find what they've been looking for.

And when they'd all been healed, every last one of them, the story says, he turned to his twelve new students, who were all standing there—some wondering if being a disciple meant they were supposed to be doing something, some wondering if they would be asked to perform miracles or if there would be a test on all this, some still trying to figure out why Jesus had picked them (a question they would ask themselves for a long time to come). He turned to those twelve fishermen and tax collectors and brothers and Zealots and traitors, and something about that moment— maybe knowing what was to come for them, maybe being overwhelmed by the pain and the joy he'd just seen—something in that moment caused him to utter words more profound and ridiculous than any the world had ever before heard.

"Blessed are the brokenhearted, the lost, the hated, the hungry, those with tears in their eyes and nothing in their pockets. And my deepest regrets to those who think they have it all, for they don't know what they're missing. They don't know their own need."

And you may be standing here, in this level place, wondering what you're doing here. Wondering what God was thinking by calling you here, wondering if a mistake hasn't been made. Wondering if there isn't something else you should be doing or saying or being, wondering if this is more of a blessing or a curse to be invited to stand beside this stranger from Nazareth.

Wherever these pages find you, whatever turn your story has taken, Christ has these words for you. They are not an instruction manual for how to live your life, because Jesus is more into on-the-job training than he is into clear and detailed instructions. They are, however, a map—a map of grace, a promise that God's love will be where the wounds of the world are, in the darkness and the hopelessness and the doubt and the pain. That there is no boundary to where God will be, that there is no place we can go, no experience we can have, no hole so deep that God will not be right there with us, blessing us even when we feel unblessable.

Christ's words to his disciples, to Peter and James and Judas and you and me, are a window into how God sees the world. The same God who created us, who knows our inner workings, our deepest hopes and fears, the number of hairs on our head—this God is the one who stands before all of us who are disheartened and incomplete, and speaks something so ridiculous, so foolish, that it must be the truest truth there ever was. It is the same strange mathematics that Paul was trying to teach the church at Corinth—that our hope, our faith, *our everything*, is built on an empty tomb, the death and life again of an executed man. It is ridiculous, it is unproven, it is not practical, but it's everything. Because it means that this same Jesus, who stands there in a level place and declares that the world is about to be leveled, that those in pain are the apple of God's eye—this same Jesus will walk into the deepest darknesses of death, to show that there is no place God's love will not be, no place God's love will not go.

So if you feel as if your story is going nowhere, as if you are stuck in the middle of nothing and nowhere, I would remind you that your story and God's story are not so different after all. That even when you find yourself in the pit of despair, when you feel the most alone, there is a character in the shadows. One you can't always see or hear, but who is always waiting for you there in the darkness. Waiting for you to discover the story that is behind all our stories, the hope that gives life even when life seems impossible.

12 Time to Go

Now about eight days after these sayings Jesus took with him Peter and John and James, and went up on the mountain to pray. And while he was praying, the appearance of his face changed, and his clothes became dazzling white. Suddenly they saw two men, Moses and Elijah, talking to him. They appeared in glory and were speaking of his departure, which he was about to accomplish at Jerusalem. Now Peter and his companions were weighed down with sleep; but since they had stayed awake, they saw his glory and the two men who stood with him. Just as they were leaving him, Peter said to Jesus, "Master, it is good for us to be here; let us make three dwellings, one for you, one for Moses, and one for Elijah"— not knowing what he said. While he was saying this, a cloud came and overshadowed them; and they were terrified as they entered the cloud. Then from the cloud came a voice that said, "This is my Son, my Chosen; listen to him!" When the voice had spoken, Jesus was found alone. And they kept silent and in those days told no one any of the things they had seen. (Luke 9:28–36)

I have an exercise I like to do with people that I stole from one of my seminary professors. I'm sure that many of you have done some variation of it—it's called a "life-line." The basic idea is that you take a piece of paper, and you draw a line that represents the ten or so most formative events of your life. It ends up looking like a really unstable stock market graph, because the events end up being split between highs and lows. The moments where things were really great, everything really clicked—those moments are marked by an upward spike in the line. But there are always an equal number of dips, where the line goes below sea level, indicating a falling away, argument, misunderstanding, or sadness. The most interesting part of the exercise is always the end, because you have to decide how your life right now measures up to the peaks and the valleys of your past. You have to decide where you are.

For a long time, I told my story using my peak moments, my time on the mountaintop, as the entire plot line. Most of us in the church have a nasty habit of doing that, because it seems that the mountaintop moments are a sort of religious credential; those of us who have spent a lot of time up there seem to be closer to God. I have some friends who can't seem to walk down a street without a bush catching on fire and telling them what they're supposed to do next. They are capable of speaking of God in such defined and definitive ways, that they might as well be talking about their uncle, instead of the Creator of the Universe. For those of us who hear God in faint echoes rather than booming broadcasts, it is enough pressure just to figure out who we are, what we're supposed to be doing with ourselves. To be in the company of people who seem to have it so clear makes the pressure divinely sanctioned. And sometimes we worry that God just isn't interested in us. We're left wondering why the bushes in our lives seem so non-flammable.

And I would imagine Peter's thoughts are not far from that this particular day, as he slowly walks behind Jesus and his friends, his sandaled feet searching for good footing as they make their way up the mountainside. Here is someone who has left everything he has, everything he knows—friends, family, a steady job where he at least knew what to expect every morning—to fall in line behind a stranger from Nazareth. To tell you the truth, most days he can't even articulate why he did it, why he dropped that net and climbed out of the boat. He just did. And ever since then, he's wondered if it would ever make sense to him—if all the sleeping on strangers' floors, moving from town to town hoping you'll get a meal that day, the recurring headaches that come from trying to figure out Jesus' stories—Peter's been wondering if it would all pay off.

And there, at the top of the hill, it seems to. In the middle of his wondering where it is they're going this time, the clouds break and the light comes through. There are suddenly two strangers speaking to Jesus. Don't ask how he knows it, but Peter knows he is standing in the company of Elijah and Moses, two others who are no strangers to the mountaintop. The voice of God speaks from the sky. Jesus lights up like a forty-billion-watt halogen, and for a moment, for just a moment, Peter feels something he has never felt before. Certainty. Clarity. Everything falls into place. And it is a good feeling.

So it's no surprise that Peter (who you may remember was born without a filter between his brain and his mouth) speaks up. "Can we stay? This is what we've been waiting for. This is what it's all about. This is what people need, the healing and the feeding and the teaching, that's all great, but what people need is just to see this, to be here, to feel like this. We can build a little park, with a booth for you and for Moses and for Elijah, and just stay here, and people can come and feel that God is real. That all this is real. Can we stay? I have to be honest with you, for a minute there I thought we were just going to walk around in circles, hanging out with sick folks, and that's great and all, but . . ."

And then the lights go out. In the middle of Peter's planning, in the middle of that bright moment of clarity and wisdom, everything changes back to normal. No voice from the clouds. No Moses. No Elijah. Jesus' coat that looked like a firecracker just a second ago looks just as ratty and beaten as it did the day before and the day before that. And before they can ask again, before they can even process what has just happened, Jesus starts back down the rocky path. "This way," he says. "There's work to do."

I don't know where you find yourself in your own story. I don't know if you're feasting on the mountain or starving in the valley. I don't know if God feels as close as your own breath or more like a distant unnamed star. But this much I do know—the life of faith is more than just clarity. It is more than just the warm and cozy moments of God's nearness. As much as we would like to think that, the life of faith is about *all* moments. The good and the bad and the indifferent. The ones that are as clear as crystal and the ones as muddy as Peter's footsteps down the mountainside.

The life of faith is about church and worship, but it is also about the world beyond the sanctuary walls. It is about reading the Bible and prayer, but it is also about being willing to stand in the middle of that hurting and broken world, and to live a life of connection and hope. The life of faith is about kindness and peace, but it is also about fighting injustice with righteous anger.

The simple truth of it is, those of us who want to stay with Jesus have to keep our bags packed. While we'd like to set up camp in the good times, you have to know that to follow Jesus is to *follow* him. Everywhere. Up onto the mountains and down into the shadows. Into the quiet moments of reflection and into the chaotic recesses of our deepest fears. Into all the comfort and all the rough edges this life can offer. And that is why you need no special qualifications, just a willingness to follow, to wake up in the morning and trust that your journey is your destination, that your calling will always be a calling, always pulling you forward, down into the valley.

So it's time to go. I wish you well on whatever awaits you down there, and I hope that you can remember that even in the foggiest of times, there is one who stands just a few steps away, always calling you forward. It's the same one who even now is making his way down off the mountain, away from these bright days of Epiphany. We'd better get moving. He seems to know where he's going.

"This way. There's work to do."

13 Lent: Trusting the Road

The horizon is clouded now.
Even if we could see, we're not sure we'd want to.
Each step demands more,
carrying us into a darkness deeper than death,
a flashlight on our wounds.
The air is thinner, as is our company.
For this is our road to walk alone.
Through no strength of our own,
step follows step follows step
deeper into deeper into deeper.
The horizon is clouded.

But we belong to the path now . . .

What can you say about Lent? It is the red-headed stepchild of the Christian year, where we parade the skeletons in our closet and walk around with ash-covered foreheads.

Most of us end up neutralizing the acridness of the season by turning it into a novelty of sacrifice, "giving up" some extraneous temptation, an act that usually results in a heightened craving for chocolate rather than God.

But no matter how we botch up the season, its mere existence is a powerful witness. There is a place for pain. There is a place for darkness. The journey of faith must weave its way through the thorns and brambles of death.

Scripturally, there is no place in the Gospels as detailed as the accounts of Jesus' walk to the cross. This story must be told, in all its horror and all its darkness, otherwise Easter Sunday is little more than pomp and circumstance, "much ado about nothing." The exclamation point of Easter makes no sense without the jagged question mark of Lent.

Historically, this was the time of preparation for new converts to the faith. It was a time of rigor and discernment, as the faithful prepared their heads and hearts for the transformation of their own lives, for taking their place in the body of Christ.

No matter how long ago our baptisms, all of us would do well to remember that without this stranger from Nazareth, we are of as much significance as the dust on his sandals. That does not mean that Lent is about self-deprecation and abuse, far from it. Lent is the time on the calendar that speaks with the greatest intensity about the power of the human spirit. As Abraham Joshua Heschel reminded us, "Our energies are too abundant for living indifferently."

For this moment that we are more than dust, what will we do? Who will we be, or maybe most importantly, *whose* will we be?

14 Packing for the Desert

Jesus, full of the Holy Spirit, returned from the Jordan and was led by the Spirit in the wilderness, where for forty days he was tempted by the devil. He ate nothing at all during those days, and when they were over, he was famished. The devil said to him, "If you are the Son of God, command this stone to become a loaf of bread." Jesus answered him, "It is written, 'One does not live by bread alone.'" Then the devil led him up and showed him in an instant all the kingdoms of the world. And the devil said to him, "To you I will give their glory and all this authority; for it has been given over to me, and I give it to anyone I please. If you, then, will worship me, it will all be yours." Jesus answered him, "It is written, 'Worship the Lord your God, and serve only him.'" Then the devil took him to Jerusalem, and placed him on the pinnacle of the temple, saying to him, "If you are the Son of God, throw yourself down from here, for it is written, 'He will command his angels concerning you, to protect you,' and 'On their hands they will bear you up, so that you will not dash your foot against a stone.'" Jesus answered him, "It is said, 'Do not put the Lord your God to the test.'" When the devil had finished every test, he departed from him until an opportune time.
(Luke 4:1–13)

It was with great expectation that I followed Jesus out here into the desert, because I wanted to know what changed for him out here. You have to remember, those of you who have spent any time with Jesus, that for about thirty years, he just didn't move. He wasn't completely still of course, but he looked more like you or me than a Messiah. He helped with the dishes. He laughed with friends and told stories. He tried to make a decent living the best way he knew how. But he didn't move, at least not enough to show up on the radar screen. For a long time, Jesus didn't move.

And your guess is as good as mine why he wakes up one day and everything changes. Why he bypasses the door to his father's shop and keeps on walking until he reaches the Jordan. Why he moves through the crowd of nobodies who are trying to decide if they want to go through with this or not, and takes his place in line. Why a very normal, very quiet Jesus steps into that cold, muddy water with his cousin John, who yells at strangers, eats locusts and wild honey, and hasn't been normal for quite some time.

Maybe if we knew why he did all that, we might better understand what he is doing here in the desert, why he walks straight from that experience of wonder and beauty, a moment where the heavens open up and God declares him "beloved" into this dry and desolate place. The writer of Luke doesn't seem to think it needs an explanation—he gets it all in one sentence: *Jesus returned from the Jordan full of the Holy Spirit and was led by the Spirit into the desert, where he was tempted by the Devil for forty days*—as if it were some sort of overly rehearsed math equation that should just make sense to us—you get baptized, you head off into the desert to hang with the Devil.

Maybe the water in the Jordan wasn't enough to wash away his old life—maybe he needed a buffer, some time apart before he started down his new road. Maybe, as the story says, he was just following the Spirit, letting it take him wherever it wanted to, and he was just as surprised as we are to be out here in this empty place.

Whatever draws him out here, this is the last step in his preparation, the last straw that pushes him over the edge, transforming a quiet life that looks like any other into a healer, teacher, Savior, Christ—the likes of which the world had never seen before. He walks in looking like anyone else, but on the other side he comes out saying things that make no sense, like "blessed are the poor," turning someone's lunch leftovers into a feast, and loving people into wholeness. Surely there is something out here in the rocky ground, in the dry wind, that might tell us what this is all about, so every year about this time we pack up our churches and we caravan ourselves out into the wilderness to set up camp, to wait, and to watch. To see if he will pass this way. To see if our questions might be answered. To see if, by staying out here on our own, by leaving the comforts of our daily lives, we too might be transformed.

So we take only what we need. In my favorite U2 song these days, "Walk On," Bono chants the phrase: "Love is not the easy thing, the only baggage you can bring is all that you can't leave behind." And that may be the best packing list for the Lenten journey I've ever heard. Because we all carry a lot of stuff in our lives. Not just material goods, though we have enough of those to merit a booming storage rental business on every corner of the city. Not just emotional baggage, priorities that go unchecked and calendars that no longer reflect our values; not just our need to be in four places at one time. And the wilderness, where nothing really thrives, is a perfect mirror for that. So we start down the Lenten road with five or six pieces of Samsonite luggage on our backs, wearing six or seven layers of clothes, because we couldn't pick just one outfit for forty days.

But pretty soon, the load lightens. It has to. It seems silly, all that we packed for a trip into nowhere. It's just not practical. Chocolate melts out here in the desert, so we put it up on the shelf. Some of us try to go without food for a day or so, starting to realize how much we took those meals for granted. We spend some time with our suffering sisters and brothers, just grateful for the company. We pray more out here, maybe because there is nothing else to do, but I suspect it has more to do with our giving our hearts enough of a break to know what to say, and more importantly, how to listen. So the longer we stay, the more infrequently we use the word "necessity" to describe our possessions, the less we find ourselves worrying that if we're fifteen minutes late to the soccer game the sky might come crashing down on our fragile lives. At least, that's the way Lent is supposed to work.

But we all know it's not that easy. Most of us, when faced with the decision to set down our luggage or turn back for home, will always choose the latter. We need our chocolate. We need our clutter. *It is who we are.* We are afraid that if we put down our distractions, if we spend time alone with ourselves, we will discover that there is nothing there. That at the core of who we are, in the deepest and darkest recesses of our hearts, we have been starving our souls for so long they have simply withered and disappeared. One writer calls Lent the time for "bright sadness," when all the wounds and all the fears are exposed by the candle of our self-reflection. It is hard to be out here, so we wonder: Why did Jesus come this way? What was God thinking by pulling him up from the currents of the Jordan into this place of loneliness and temptation?

I have often read this story picturing a Jesus who just coasts through these temptations, as though he's got a copy of the script. Most people don't like to think about Jesus' humanity. Those of us who spend time in the church are much more comfortable with Jesus' divinity, the part that makes him different from us. It is far too frightening to talk about the overlaps between this stranger from Nazareth and those of us who live in the real world. We want a superhero who lets us off the hook, not someone who models wholeness and compassion, because that might mean that we risk making the same choices, that we hold in our lives the possibility of abundant life. So most of the time we focus on how Jesus is different from us. No stars hung in the sky at my birth. No shepherds showed up at St. Vincent's Hospital to wish my parents well. No birds descended from the rafters at Vestavia Hills United Methodist when I was baptized.

But this story, Jesus' time apart, his walking alone in the desert—this story falls into the overlap. This story is about us. To understand why Jesus has come out here, you will have to set aside all your superhero images of him. He has no cape. He has no superhuman capacity to feel God's presence. He feels just as alone as we do out here. His stomach rumbles just like ours. His tongue sticks to the roof of his mouth. His skin is just as chafed by the wind as our own. But maybe the most painful suffering he endures out here is his broken heart—he feels, in that deep recess of his soul, that he is alone. That he has been abandoned. Maybe it is not the first time he's felt like this; it will certainly not be the last.

And so when the voice of the tempter sounds in his ear, the voice that sounds less like a dragon and more like our own, the temptation is real. The temptation to satisfy his hunger. To have what he wants right now, to give up the chance of satisfying his real need for the sake of meeting his immediate desire. The temptation to have control, even if it means sacrificing what he believes in. This is a dark and lonely place that Christ finds himself in, and he must find the answers for himself. He must search that painful place, deep within his own heart, to find strength to make his way through. For a moment out here, without food or water or a companion, he must live only on his faith, a faith that can't be seen or quantified, a faith that can't be rationally explained or understood.

And it is that faith that carries him through the third and deepest temptation, the temptation to prove himself, the temptation to be something he is not. The Devil even quotes scripture here, proving that just because you know the Bible doesn't mean you know what the life of faith is about. And there, in that moment of darkness, Jesus of Nazareth becomes Jesus the Christ. Because he discovers that even at the end of his rope, at the edge of utter exhaustion and abandonment, in a place where it seems that life cannot exist, there is one more character in his story: God. Even when he is broken, when he has nothing left to stand on, God is with him. He was never alone.

And there is the transformation. Because knowing that, he is now ready to walk the path that lies before him. A path that leads to a garbage heap outside of town, where they brutally murder criminals, where his friends will desert him, where his body will be broken and bent by hatred and darkness. But he will go there anyway, not because he won't feel the pain, not because he won't feel the fear, but because he learned something out here in the desert, out here in these days of waiting and uncertainty. He learned that the same God who was with him at birth, who watched over him in those quiet years, who spoke of his belovedness at the Jordan, and who walked with him through the wilderness of temptation— that same God will never leave his side. He will not always be able to see it, he will not always be able to feel it, but when everything else has melted away and it seems that there is no ground for hope, God is there.

Welcome to this Lenten path. I warn you, it goes into some dark places. It will take you into feelings and fears you do not feel ready for, but I have checked the map as many times as you have, and there is no other road to life. For the strange mystery of God is that God appears more often in the waiting rooms of our lives than in the temples, in the deserts instead of the sanctuaries. So pack your bags. You can't take much. Only that which you can't leave behind—the grace and company of a God who loves you beyond measure.

15 Where Your Feet Take You

"Do not store up for yourselves treasures on earth, where moth and rust consume and where thieves break in and steal; but store up for yourselves treasures in heaven, where neither moth nor rust consumes and where thieves do not break in and steal. For where your treasure is, there your heart will be also."
(Matthew 6:19–21)

My favorite author, Frederick Buechner, writes that "if you want to know who you are, watch your feet. Because where your feet take you, that is who you are." We find ourselves at a crossroads of sorts. Behind us is the glory of Christmas and the Epiphany, when angels hung in the sky, God spoke from the clouds, and Jesus began to look and act and talk the way we thought a Messiah should. We are fresh from that place, the brilliance of it all still burned in our memory. We long for God to say something clear again, give us some direction. For Jesus to do something amazing that we can gape in awe about, something that will make us sleep better at night. We long for the mountain again, where Jesus was revealed to be light itself, where he seemed relaxed for a change, not so focused on Jerusalem. That was a good place.

But it seems that the more time we spend with this Jesus, the more we realize he is not the person we thought he was. We lost him for a moment coming down the mountain. In the confusion and excitement, he must have slipped away. Something inside of us knew that if we let him get away, he would head back this way. South toward Jerusalem. And against our better judgment, we tried to follow him. Thinking that maybe we could stop him, talk some sense into him. He can be so stubborn when he sets his mind to something. And so here we are, staring down this road to Jerusalem.

It is time to begin this strange journey, time to answer for ourselves the question of who we are, of where we will allow our feet to take us. Our bags are packed, which means that we have emptied them. Our company is all here, for we know that this narrow path is ours to walk alone. As we glance over the map, staring at the thin line that does not waver across the page, our minds race with all the other ways. All the shortcuts. All the smoother roads. But we have seen him. It was just a shadow, hardly even a glimpse, but we saw him. And this is the way he was walking.

But there is still a voice inside of us that says we have had enough. Enough dust. Enough death. Enough pain. This is his road to walk, not ours. Put a blessing on our heads, not ashes. God must know that we have had enough ashes. Our lungs are still black from Ground Zero. Our ears are still ringing with the bombs dropped in response. We get it—the world is broken. We have had enough destruction. Don't make us walk this way. We cannot go any further.

The part of us that can still think is wrapped up in all the things we have left behind. There is so much back there. So much that calmed the anxiety, pacified the unrest, soothed our weariness. Admittedly, it never quite filled the hole, but as long as we couldn't see it, we could pretend it wasn't there. If we rearranged the furniture enough, if we worked hard enough to fill up all our hours with busyness and distraction, if we took what was ultimately unimportant as crucial, everything was okay. It didn't matter if we didn't understand why we did the things we did; what was important was that we did them—right? We are happy to look into a mirror, but to stare into the depths of our souls, that is too much to ask, too great a burden to bear. But something tells us that out here, on the road to the nowhere that leads to an end we cannot imagine, it is our hearts now that are at stake. It is who we are, not what we do or say, that matters now. We can no longer hide behind the little things. But the question remains—when they are unraveled, what will be left?

And in the end, that will be what carries us on. The thing that remains. When all else is ashes, when everything else is taken away, Lent is the promise that there will still be something worth living for. When we are enveloped in darkness, somewhere a candle still burns. It might be hard to see. It is certainly elusive. It does not announce itself on billboards or shout for our attention. And that is why this season, this journey, will be so hard. It is not that Lent is a sad time in and of itself, it is that this road is like a flashlight, making visible what was always there, calling our attention to the parts of ourselves we only whisper about, our deepest shame, our deepest fears, the people inside of us we would discard if ever given the chance. And in that self-aware sadness, we are called to walk on. To follow. To give our hearts, not just our discipline. To give our time, not just our schedules. To give ourselves over to this mysterious man, who is always as much a stranger as he is our friend. Trusting that, in the end, to give up everything is to gain all, and that there is cause for rejoicing even in the darkest of our days.

So if you want to know who you are, watch your feet. But be cautious, for if you are not careful, you will find that your steps are his, and that the road does not so much lead somewhere as the road itself is somewhere. In the end, there is not any clear decision we can make. At best, it is desperation or confusion or hunger that makes us keep going. Not knowing where you belong gives you permission to keep searching. Keep going. Keep wandering. Watch your feet.

16 Living with a Living God

Then God said to Noah and to his sons with him, "As for me, I am establishing my covenant with you and your descendants after you, and with every living creature that is with you, the birds, the domestic animals, and every animal of the earth with you, as many as came out of the ark. I establish my covenant with you, that never again shall all flesh be cut off by the waters of a flood, and never again shall there be a flood to destroy the earth."
(Genesis 9:8–11)

In those days Jesus came from Nazareth of Galilee and was baptized by John in the Jordan. And just as he was coming up out of the water, he saw the heavens torn apart and the Spirit descending like a dove on him. And a voice came from heaven, "You are my Son, the Beloved; with you I am well pleased."

And the Spirit immediately drove him out into the wilderness. He was in the wilderness forty days, tempted by Satan; and he was with the wild beasts; and the angels waited on him. (Mark 1:9–13)

The problem with the Bible is that it doesn't come in installments, so we end up chopping it up to fit our needs. Most of us enjoy some parts of Jesus' life, almost all of us have favorite books or stories from the Bible—things that speak to us, make sense to us, help us with our faith. And in this consumerist culture, we really don't know how to do any different. We stick with what we like. Our president recently reiterated a statement from his State of the Union address, that liberty is God's gift to humanity. We are in charge of our own development. Choices are always good. Doesn't that make sense?

Chances are, at some point in your life you will "pick a church," much like you pick out an outfit at the mall. You will find something that fits, that gives you some sense of comfort, where the music is pleasing to you and they have good donuts. Even after all that, you will find yourself more likely to describe that place as "the church that I attend" rather than "my church," because you'll always be re-evaluating whether or not you really want to commit yourself to this place. If you can't find something you like, or some place you agree with, you won't buy the outfit.

We do the same thing with our own theologies. Everyone has a theology, a way of understanding God, whether or not you've ever sat down and thought about it. We all approach God with different baggage, sometimes creating God out of our own images, to like what we like and hate who we hate. And that is much easier to do if you stay away from the portions of the Bible, the parts of the story, that don't jibe with yours. I would like it very much if I could edit the Bible and take out all the places where women are sexually abused, where racial politics are enthusiastically promoted, where God calls for war, where Jesus calls that woman a "dog"—all the things that don't fit in my puzzle.

There are enough of those things in the Bible, if you really read the whole thing, to make a lot of sensible people give up altogether. This doesn't fit. I don't agree with that. This is not for me. Or the other alternative, which is simply to ignore the parts of the Bible that don't agree with your theology. The church has been pretty good about that over its history, killing innocent women, men, and children because they were infidels; keeping blacks out of the white churches and in poverty. Even now, as the modern church argues over issues like homosexuality, abortion, and economic injustice, it becomes a matter of who can fire off the most one-liners from scripture. And when we let ourselves fall into that trap, the Bible no longer has anything to say. When it becomes a louder version of our own voice, there is no room left for transformation, no space left in the air for proclaiming good news that is hard to hear. And we never take the time to wrestle with the pieces that don't fit in our puzzle.

One of the things I've been doing lately is to listen to the local "contemporary Christian" radio station, because I think I am way too intolerant of contemporary Christian music, and that's something I want to work on. And after a few hours of listening, I could think of a lot of reasons people would turn to that station. It felt positive, the songs were easy to learn because they all used pretty much the same words and tunes—it was very welcoming. But at the same time, they were all a little *too* positive. It's more than a little escapist, whitewashing the ambiguities and struggles of faith with repetitive choruses that hypnotize more than they energize. At some point, good theology has to wrestle with gang violence and poverty and malnutrition and biomedical ethics, and that means good worship has to do all those things as well.

We read in Genesis about the great flood, and no doubt many of us grew up with images of Noah and all the cutesy little animals marching onto the boat, two by two. At the church where I worked in Atlanta, we gave children's Bibles to all the third-graders, and on the cover was a precious little picture of Noah and family, smiling for the camera along with their brightly colored animal friends. I imagine a less popular version of the children's Bible with millions of frightened people drowning under the wrath of an angry and vengeful God. See if that makes it into any nursery décor. But it's part of the story—it's at least half of the story, and we have to be willing to wrestle with that piece of it, too, or else it is just a story.

The rainbow that God gives, the promise never to let this happen again, can only be understood when you remember the unimaginable life that was lost, the creation that was both shaped by and destroyed by God's own hands. The rainbow's bright promise only makes sense in the shadow of that flood. The toughest part about that story when you take it at face value is that it seems as though God made a mistake—we can argue about when and what the mistake was, whether it was letting things get so out of hand in the first place or destroying all of humanity except Noah and his family. But God's promise to never, ever let this happen again—to write this promise so grandly across the sky so that there will be no mistake—is hard for me to interpret in any other way than God learning something new. God growing.

And so we shouldn't be too surprised when God's Son acts so strangely. Rather than come down to earth and march straight to the cross and get it all over with, as a good action hero would, Jesus takes the time to grow into who he must finally be. It seems ridiculous that Jesus would even consider being baptized—it seems like overkill for the Son of God to need to receive grace. And then when he chooses to be baptized, it is not in the temple where it would be proper, by card-carrying clergy—it is out here in the nasty Jordan River, standing in line like all the other sinners, waiting his turn to be dunked underwater by this social outcast who eats bugs and wears shirts that intentionally give him a rash. But sure enough, as soon as Jesus gets his turn, holding his nose and going under like all the rest, the same God who made the rainbow thousands of years before, looks upon this act of solidarity and whispers something like—"That's my boy."

But there is no potluck supper to follow Jesus' baptism, there are no handshakes or congratulations, no one dresses him up in a nice white outfit—they hardly even get the chance to say anything to him, because the same God that seemed so pleased with him, so affirming at his baptism, that same God sends him immediately into a desert, where he is surrounded by hungry animals that are not quite as photogenic or friendly as those on the cover of a third-grader's Bible. And this will not be the last time Jesus is shoved back and forth from shadow to spotlight—he will spend the rest of his precious few days on Earth being jostled back and forth between the highest of praises and the most murderous of angers. It seems that this is part of what it means to be a Savior, part of what it means to be fully human and fully divine.

Be careful when you say that God is love, because to say this is also to concede that God is about change. That God is not the stable, unchanging, definable quality that you can set your coffee cup on or set your watch by. To say that God is Eternal is not so much to say that if you take a picture of God now, you can take the exact same picture 5,000 years from now—it is to say that the thing that lasts is growth. To say that God rested on the seventh day but then got up bright and early on the eighth and started this creation thing all over again. To say that the Good Book contains truth and life and light is to admit that the pages and words are not the final say, but instead they are the springboard for us into this crazy dynamic story that we are still trying to sort out. We should treat this book with reverence—not the kind you show for a nice piece of furniture, but the kind you show for an M-80 firecracker.

To be willing to engage in this Lenten journey is to open these closets inside of us that are full of skeletons and ghosts, truths that we are too ashamed or afraid to claim as true. But to open them, to be honest about them, is to draw near to God. To be in this Lenten journey is to remember that our baptism is not so much about the grace we choose, but the grace that chooses us. If we are willing to ride out the flood, to make a path through this desert, to put aside our own need to choose and instead be chosen for once, we will find that we, too, are characters in this ongoing story of life and heartbreak and redemption. That God is as unpredictable and unexplainable as the heartbeat that stirs within your chest. Draw near to God in these forty days, but don't expect to stand still.

17 Telling the Story Backwards

Then he began to teach them that the Son of Man must undergo great suffering, and be rejected by the elders, the chief priests, and the scribes, and be killed, and after three days rise again. He said all this quite openly. And Peter took him aside and began to rebuke him. But turning and looking at his disciples, he rebuked Peter and said, "Get behind me, Satan! For you are setting your mind not on divine things but on human things." He called the crowd with his disciples, and said to them, "If any want to become my followers, let them deny themselves and take up their cross and follow me. For those who want to save their life will lose it, and those who lose their life for my sake, and for the sake of the gospel, will save it. For what will it profit them to gain the whole world and forfeit their life? Indeed, what can they give in return for their life? Those who are ashamed of me and of my words in this adulterous and sinful generation, of them the Son of Man will also be ashamed when he comes in the glory of his Father with the holy angels." (Mark 8:31–38)

A funny thing happens when you tell a story backwards. If you think about it, all good storytellers work backwards from the end. They know where they've got to get you, so they start, really, with the ending. All the little turns and nuances from the beginning of the story through the middle are just to make sure you end up where they want you to, because the point, the punch line, is always there waiting for you.

And the Gospels are no different. Scholars believe that of all four Gospels, Mark is by far the oldest, but even Mark is much younger than most of the rest of the New Testament. Most researchers believe that Mark was written at least half a century after Jesus died. Not that the story wasn't already being told before then—in fact, there are scrap pieces of other Gospels that never made it into the Bible. The stories were never forgotten, they were just passed on orally within families and faith communities. Figuring that Jesus would be back before dinner time, the earliest Christians didn't see much need to record the stories formally. The traditions about Jesus and his life were so rich—how would you even begin to concretize such a dynamic, living narrative?

The point is, when the author of Mark sat down to record his Gospel, he had a lot to work with—many stories of Jesus' miracles, the testimonies of his friends, and an especially detailed account of the end. Of all the stories that survived about Jesus, it was the story about his end that remained the most intact—the best-preserved piece of his life was his death. That is why most of Matthew, Mark, and Luke have Jesus running around from place to place with seemingly no direction or commentary, and then suddenly the story about his last week on Earth is so detailed. When Mark sat down to tell this story, the most important story ever told, he started with the ending.

And in a lot of ways, when we sit down to read this story, any of these biblical stories, we also start out knowing how it's going to turn out. We don't expect to turn to the end of the book and find out that Jesus decided against the cross in favor of opening a hot dog stand. We know what's coming, and that gives us a bit of comfort.

What we have to keep telling ourselves is that the others, the characters in the story who really lived it, did not have a copy of the script. And you get the feeling, if there had been a script, Jesus would have just ignored it. Every minute with him, every decision, seems like it came out of nowhere. Maybe that is why he never gave the disciples very explicit instructions for how to live their lives—he knew they would hold on to them too tightly, missing the point altogether. Instead, he kept saying, "Follow me. This way. Try and keep up. I know where I'm going."

And most of the time, that is fine for the disciples. Not that it is easy to give up the routine and rhythm of normal life to follow some vagabond all over the countryside, but Jesus seemed to have something that they desperately needed. Not that they could tell you what that was—maybe they wouldn't even have expressed it in that way, but they trusted him in a way they had never trusted anyone or anything before in their lives. Here was an answer. *The* answer. And all we have to do is follow him. Easy enough.

Until today. Unbeknownst to the disciples, they are smack dab in the middle of the story. Chapter eight of sixteen, the breaking point. There is a curve coming up in the road—and they cannot imagine what awaits them around the bend. Things are about to change.

It began simply enough. Over breakfast, Jesus heard some of them whispering about things they had heard while in town. People were always talking about Jesus, wherever they went. Everybody seemed to see in him whatever they needed to see: Moses or Elijah or some new prophet or a cure or hope or direction or an answer. Whatever people needed most, in the darkest places in their hearts, the places they could not speak about or even understand, that's what they found when they caught Jesus' eye. And so, as the disciples processed their last journey together, even as they began their next one to Caesarea Philippi, they compared notes.

Now usually, Jesus let them talk. He rarely even seemed to notice they were there, to tell you the truth. His eyes were always on the road ahead, as if he could see farther than any of them. He seemed transfixed by his forward direction most of the time, but not today. They all jumped a bit when he spoke. "Who are they saying that I am?" After an awkward silence, they all spoke at once: "John the Baptist. Elijah. I heard someone say you were a prophet."

They walked on for what seemed like hours before he spoke again: "Who do you say that I am?" This time the answer came fast—Peter had known for some time but didn't know how or when to say it, or even who to say it to, but it suddenly flowed out of him as naturally as all the other outbursts—"You're it. The promise. The Messiah. It's you."

Now in a moment like that I would like to tell you that there were fireworks and celebrations and fatted calves and all the other great things that go with really great discoveries. But there weren't. Instead of anything they might have expected, Jesus warned them to tell no one. And here in that turning point, he began to tell them about the road ahead. About what he had seen on the horizon, about what had been written on his heart ever since he was in the wilderness alone, underwater at his baptism, even being held by his mother as a child. This road was leading to darkness. To death. To a cross. That's where he was taking them.

But when Peter pulled him aside to talk him out of it—to tell him that if he was trying to motivate the troops, this was not the most convincing way—Jesus told him to get behind him. He knew where the road led. He drew the crowd around him to tell them, too, that if they wanted to be a follower, these were the terms. No more, no less. Find your cross. Pick it up, and come with me.

At some point, we have a decision to make. It is not as simple as one moment, or one prayer, or one action, but then again maybe it is. At some point, we have to decide what road we will take, whose steps we will follow. Sometimes the best way to begin is to start with the ending.

18 Dinner Party at the Crossroads

Six days before the Passover Jesus came to Bethany, the home of Lazarus, whom he had raised from the dead. There they gave a dinner for him. Martha served, and Lazarus was one of those at the table with him. Mary took a pound of costly perfume made of pure nard, anointed Jesus' feet, and wiped them with her hair. The house was filled with the fragrance of the perfume. But Judas Iscariot, one of his disciples (the one who was about to betray him), said, "Why was this perfume not sold for three hundred denarii and the money given to the poor?" (He said this not because he cared about the poor, but because he was a thief; he kept the common purse and used to steal what was put into it.) Jesus said, "Leave her alone. She bought it so that she might keep it for the day of my burial. You always have the poor with you, but you do not always have me." (John 12:1–8)

The road is about to split.

No one knows that better than the characters gathered for dinner this evening. They are all at something of a crossroads as they stare across the table at one another.

There is the host of the meal, Lazarus, who has just days before been raised from the dead by Jesus. Having never been raised from the dead before, and not knowing anyone who has, I can only imagine what that does to your perspective on—well, everything. I am thinking that the person who walked out of that tomb is quite different from the one who was carried in. We can only guess what has been racing through Lazarus's head these past few days, but no doubt there is much for him to ponder as he takes his place along-side Jesus.

And while I have never been raised from the dead, we have all probably lost a loved one. We all know something of that deep pain when a person who is unusually significant to you is tugged from your side, so Mary and Martha are understandably a bit shaken up. They have been on quite the emotional roller coaster—losing their brother, then unexpectedly gaining him back—and they are unsure if this meal is a funeral dinner or a birthday party. Psalm 126 speaks of people sowing tears only to reap joy, and Mary and Martha are powerful reminders for all of us that the jump from weeping to cel-ebration is not always the easiest of transitions.

Along with the other disciples, Judas is here. A name that reminds us at once of all that is broken inside of us, all that we hate about ourselves, all the places we are afraid to go alone. On the eve of betraying his friend and teacher, Judas has just secretly learned of the price that has been put on Jesus' head. And regardless of what you think of Judas and the choices he will make, the one thing we know for certain about him is that he was torn. In the worst way, he was torn. Not a one of us can say what made him sell out his hero for a paltry sum of money, but the brokenness inside of each one of us knows very well what it is that made him take his own life upon realizing what he had done. Judas quietly takes his place at the table with the others.

And finally, at the head of the table sits the guest of honor. Who, against better judgment has made his way back to this home in Bethany, only miles from Jerusalem, where his detractors have gathered to plot his destruction. Who, against better judgment, has raised his table companion Lazarus from the dead—a decision that will seal his pending fate. He has heard the rumors, as have his disciples, who have urged him to listen to his better judgment. And, to their frustration, he has not. Again.

This will be, he must know, his last meal outside of Jerusalem. His last meal with this family who has been so supportive of him, so invested in him even when it meant they too would be dragged down this frightening road alongside him. It is only days before Passover, only moments before he makes his way into the town of his death. In the coming week, he will be surrounded by the temporary praise of the masses, which will soon enough give way to the louder shouts of anger and confusion that will be the last sounds his human ears hear. Sitting there at the head of the table, Jesus is at a crossroads.

And to be honest, he has been for every moment of his life. If anyone knows the height and depth of human experience, it is this humble carpenter from Nazareth. He has had his life threatened, has been spat upon and ignored, only to be called Son of God the very next moment. Jesus' life and ministry have been a series of ironies. A king born in a barn. A child wiser than the eldest teacher. A voice for God unwelcome in the Temple. A prophet accompanied not by priests, but by women and fishermen.

And the scripture lessons have reminded us of that, constantly drawing our attention not only to Jesus, but to the people around him who are closing in. Closing in with their anger, their misunderstanding, their need for stability in an insecure world. Jesus pushes all of their buttons, and that is enough to warrant his death. We read of these characters with a certain naïveté, believing that we are somehow qualitatively different from all those who would want Jesus to be silent. But of course, the truth of it is that we are them and they are us. The same confusions and frustrations live inside of us that pull these characters in so many violent directions.

And so as we take our seat at this table, we too are uncertain of our place. We have many things we think we would like to say, but no words to say them. We have questions to ask, but our fear that there might not be answers for them keeps us silent. Like the rest, we just watch.

And like the rest, we are some mixture of shock and confusion when Mary moves to Jesus' feet. The same feet she fell at when her brother died, anointing them with her tears, an event so moving it even brought tears to Jesus' eyes.

75

But before anyone can say a word about the strangeness of the moment, it becomes even stranger. There is a fragrance so strong that your eyes begin to water, so strong Peter begins to sneeze, a smell so strong the only thing you have to compare it to is the smell of Lazarus's empty tomb. But this is not the scent of death, it is very much the scent of life. And as Mary slowly wipes the feet she has touched before, the feet that will be broken with cold steel only days later, you are as speechless as you have been every moment since you left what you knew to be with this one you hoped to know.

We can spend a lot of time and energy trying to figure out what motivates Mary or for that matter, Judas, or for that matter any one of us, to do what we do, say what we say. We can talk for hours about what it is about this man Jesus that makes tax collectors leave their desks, fishermen leave their boats, women to pour perfume onto his feet, and us to reluctantly step into the shadows of Lent and uncertainty. But in the end, none of it will make much sense. Our better judgment will never lead us down his path. The truth of it is—this Jesus, this nobody about whom nothing makes much sense—well, it is mostly foolishness. When Judas pipes up about the poor, he is only reciting words that he has heard Jesus himself say—he is doing his best to follow by the rules, color within the lines, make sense of what in the end is senseless.

It is only Mary, as unstable and confused as the rest of the table, who is able to take her chances on this moment. To take the chance that this will be her only chance. Not because she has something figured out that the rest don't, not because this moment is any less risky for her than the others, but because there is something deep inside of her that says she must choose. On this end of her emotional roller coaster, against better judgment, she chooses to love this man Jesus, this man who has brought her as much pain as joy, as much turmoil as comfort. She washes the feet that will, in a few days, take the final steps to a cross on top of a garbage heap, an unlikely throne for an unlikely king.

The road splits, and Mary chooses the risk, chooses the ambiguity, chooses the Christ. The road is about to split for all of us. May we too be granted the courage to fumble our way behind this strange king.

19　The Hour Has Come

Now among those who went up to worship at the festival were some Greeks. They came to Philip, who was from Bethsaida in Galilee, and said to him, "Sir, we wish to see Jesus." Philip went and told Andrew; then Andrew and Philip went and told Jesus. Jesus answered them, "The hour has come for the Son of Man to be glorified. Very truly, I tell you, unless a grain of wheat falls into the earth and dies, it remains just a single grain; but if it dies, it bears much fruit. Those who love their life lose it, and those who hate their life in this world will keep it for eternal life. Whoever serves me must follow me, and where I am, there will my servant be also. Whoever serves me, the Father will honor. Now my soul is troubled. And what should I say—'Father, save me from this hour'? No, it is for this reason that I have come to this hour. Father, glorify your name."
(John 12:20–28)

Whereas we use only one word to signify the chronological movement of history and how long something takes and our own sense of experience, the Greeks used two words, *chronos* and *kairos*. Chronos is the word for time that can be plotted out on one of those timelines you used to make in sixth-grade social studies class. It is the time that fits on your watch, that keeps your sitcoms

77

in order, that helps you set your Tivo. It is Daylight Savings Time and Palm Pilots and Dayplanners. That is chronos time.

The other kind of time, kairos, does not so easily stay within the lines. It is less about length and more about depth. It is about the quality of time. It is what you mean when you say, "I had the best time" or "That was a waste of time." It is time that is defined and shaped by the events that happen during it. It makes us say, "That was the longest day" or "I'll never forget that moment." It is why we celebrate people's birthdays—not because there is something scientifically different or philosophically unique about that particular space on the calendar, but the person whose life we remember on that day gives it a depth, a character, that makes us want to wear silly hats and blow out candles and eat cake. Kairos is also the thing that happens when we remember certain moments that are burned into our memory—like the death of a loved one or where we were when we heard about the planes crashing into those buildings in Manhattan or when we first realized we were in love. It catches you in the car, making you weep over a song that you know is stupid and isn't about what you're feeling but somehow it is, and it sneaks up on you and breaks your heart and reminds you what love is and what's most important to you and then as quickly as it came it's gone again. It is what the writer of Jeremiah means when he says, "The days are surely coming," and what Jesus is saying when he keeps whispering, "The hour has come." These are not so much "mark your calendars because you can't miss this sale of a lifetime"—they are more "mark your hearts and watch the skies and breathe more deeply." Kairos is the time that tells you when you are just passing time or when you are really living out the moments that will tell your story.

And when we gather together for worship, reading out of that old book, singing songs, sitting in silence, listening to someone reflect or pray or play the flute, we stand at the gap between chronos and kairos. I would imagine there are some of us in both places. There are some of us who are thinking of all the things that have to somehow fit into the next few hours. They are scanning their bulletin for how many things are left on the program before it's over and the next thing on their agenda starts. Or they are so mentally and emotionally exhausted that they are just going through their weekly motions, and this is what they do on Sunday mornings because it's their job or their friends are here or maybe they don't even know why.

There are others who are so caught up in the events of their lives or in the lives of their loved ones that chronos time doesn't make much sense to them anymore. They are too caught up in kairos, and each day feels like the last one. These days have a real weight to them, a heaviness that is increasingly hard to bear, and they have come seeking some relief. Maybe you are missing someone, and so the time seems to almost creep along, making the distance between you and the next time you'll see them seem like a heartbreakingly overwhelming hike that you're not sure you can make.

Wherever and when-ever you are, whether your watch is keeping you in chronos or your heart is beating with kairos, we gather because we are trying to live into *his* time. We read these stories not because we think they're better than the other stories we could be reading, but because we hope that maybe a word or a saying will break through the shell of our chronos living and we will, even if just for a moment, see the face of God. We drag ourselves back to these stories again and again in this Lenten season, following this stranger from Nazareth to his death. And even though we know what is going to happen, even though in the back of our minds we can finish the story in our sleep, we are still surprised every year that he keeps walking. It would be easier for us to watch if he acted numb to it all, if it seemed like he didn't feel it. We do much better around people that mask their pain well—we tend to reward that. It would be easier for us if he marched into it all like a madman or a superhero and didn't seem to already feel the nails that would pierce his flesh or the hatred that would fill his ears.

But with every step closer to Jerusalem, his feet become heavier. The path becomes steeper. The stakes get higher. Even before the cross has been built, even before the charges have been fabricated, he has begun to die. And this first death may be the more painful of the two, the more lonely of the two, because this is the moment of choice for him. He must will every step, knowing that each one brings him closer to the end of this road. It is the kairos moment that will determine the chronos that is to come. And as he walks with his friends, looking into their faces and seeing their misunderstanding and wanting at least one of them to understand, wishing in his heart of hearts that he could speak to someone—anyone—about his fear, his anxiety—his loneliness grows.

And so do the signs. Earlier in the chapter, Mary takes a pound of perfume and wipes his feet with her hair. It seems inappropriate, not just because of the wasted perfume and the ridiculous expense but because of the intimacy of it that scares everyone else in the room. Then he rides into town on a donkey surrounded by the cheering and confused crowd that so desperately wants a hero, they are willing to accept even someone who looks too much like them and rides not on a stallion but a borrowed donkey. And tonight, when his friends come to tell him that some Greeks want to see him, he can't even hear their request. "The hour has come. It is time. The seed has to die in order to give life, but still, I am scared to do what I know I must do. I am scared, but to stop walking now is to stop being who I am." He might as well have been speaking Swahili to them, because they couldn't see what he could see. They were still standing there in chronos time, not realizing how little of it they had left to spend with him.

The hour has come. Not all will realize what it means or what is happening, even some of us who show up in our Easter best to put flowers on the cross out on the church lawn. In these final days, try to resist the temptation to finish the story yourself. Instead, let the story say what it must, let it tell itself again for the first time. As much as your heart wants to race ahead to Easter, out of this awkward and heavy time, away from the burdens of war and the stress of these days, stay here with Jesus. Walk at his pace. Live at his rhythm. Because there is something funny about the chemistry of human life: the moments that will mean the most, where you will know yourself best, do not come when we plan them on the calendar. They come in the awkward unpredictability of labor pains and sudden tragic death and falling in love. They come at the table where Christ shares bread and wine, telling us as we eat and drink them that he is inside us and we are inside him and there can be no further explanation. They are the moments that come when we are willing to follow this scared wanderer wherever he leads us, into the heart of the darkness and the pain of war and the heat of the fire and the end of our old road. The hour has come. In these hours we have been given, may we have the audacity to recognize the moments that matter, and the courage to believe that all of them do.

20 The First Supper

For I received from the Lord what I also handed on to you, that the Lord Jesus on the night when he was betrayed took a loaf of bread, and when he had given thanks, he broke it and said, "This is my body that is for you. Do this in remembrance of me." In the same way he took the cup also, after supper, saying, "This cup is the new covenant in my blood. Do this, as often as you drink it, in remembrance of me." For as often as you eat this bread and drink the cup, you proclaim the Lord's death until he comes. (1 Corinthians 11:23–26)

When Jesus gathers them for supper, they do not know it will be the last one. As they take their places around the table as they have done so many times before, they have no idea what the next few hours will hold. After all the parables and miracles and storms they have witnessed by now, they know enough to expect the unexpected. But as they sit down to enjoy that fateful meal together, everything seems pretty normal. For those of us peeking in on the scene, well, we know what they could not have known—that there was nothing normal about this supper. Every minute, every breath, draws them closer to the end of the way things have been. But only one of them knows that, and for the rest, it could not have been a more ordinary occasion.

By now, they are quite used to each other. They know each other's stories, they know each other's dreams. By now, they know the sound of each other's laughter, the way Peter turns red when he's upset, the silly look Judas gets on his face when he's embarrassed. By now, they are friends.

You should know if you don't already that this wasn't always the case—they began as strangers. They came from different places, different families, they had different stories to tell. Some of them left fishing boats. Some stood up and walked away from tax collectors' booths. All of them left something. Families. Dreams. Familiarity. Stability. All of them left something because of the one thing—maybe the only thing—they had in common: *Him.*

And while each of them dropped everything to follow this man from Nazareth, not one of them could tell you exactly why they did it. Not that they wouldn't try, but their answers would vary depending on when you asked them and who you happened to ask. Peter might try to give an explanation, just because Peter is that way, always willing to give an answer even if it's the wrong one. But, truth be told, not one of them around the table could tell you exactly why they dropped their nets and closed up shop that day, choosing to give up everything in order to do that one thing, taking the path that led to who-knows-where, deciding that their steps made the most sense in line with his, wherever he happened to be going.

It's not that he said anything especially unusual or persuasive. He certainly made no promises. If anything, most of his promises sounded more like threats. He didn't happen to mention where they were going, didn't give them the pros and cons for taking his path. There was no dental plan involved, and he made no attempt to tell them why it was they should follow him. At least no attempt they understood. Whenever they asked him for clarity on any of these things, he was always replying with some nonsense story about a fig or a mustard seed or some sheep that keeps getting lost. Not particularly helpful. So why did they leave everything—all that they knew and loved and understood—for a place at this table?

Maybe it was his eyes. The way he looked at you, well, you just can't explain away something like that. It was as if he could see through you—into the best and worst and happiest and saddest, into the most fearless and most fearful—and still smile back.

Maybe it was his touch. Those who gathered around the table that night had all been beaten up by life too many times to count, too many times to ever trust anyone again. At least that's what they used to think. Whenever he touched someone, it was if they had seen a ghost or an angel or some combination of both—as if for the first time they understood that their life really mattered. It's the healing of blindness and sickness and leprosy that gets all the press, but for those around the table, the real miracle was in the way that those who had been healed went on to act . . . like him.

Maybe it was his voice. The way he spoke your name, calling you to be everything you had ever been and more, calling you to be at home inside your skin while feeling as if you were about to explode in it at the same time.

I suppose there are as many reasons for us being here as there are places around the table. Some of us were looking for hope when he wandered down our way. Some of us were searching for love, and he spoke a kind word, the word we needed and didn't even know. Some of us don't know what it is we were looking for; we still can't tell you, but we know somehow that he is the end of our search. And so we dropped everything. Everything. Because we thought we saw him coming this way. We left behind the easy and the familiar and the comfortable for a chance to fall in step with his path. To have a place at this table with him, with each other.

And just as it was for the disciples, there is change headed our way too. We can't put our finger on it, but we know that in a matter of hours or days our world, too, will change. And our hearts, like theirs, will break because it will seem as if we are suddenly alone. As if our community has ended, as if he has drawn us out here only to slip out when we weren't looking. For some of us it will feel as if our dreams were only dreams, and we will awkwardly return to our homes, no longer feeling as if we fit inside our own lives. Fearing that it will never be the same—maybe that is the greatest fear of all, the one that tells us no one will understand what has happened here, that no one will believe what our eyes have seen, that these promises we have made to ourselves and God will fade away. We are afraid that this has all been in vain, and we will have to face whatever it is that comes next alone.

But then, just when we convince ourselves that our worst fears have won, that this has all come crashing to an end, Jesus stands up. He takes the bread, says a prayer, and breaks off a piece for each of us, reminding us that while we were once strangers, we're now a part of the same whole. A piece of the same puzzle. And as he makes his way around the table to each of us, he stops, smiles, and says something, the gist of which is this: "Things are about to change, and it is going to feel as if I am very far away, as if this family we have made has disappeared. But every time you sit down around the table, every time you feel a hunger inside you for something more, every time you share bread with one another, remember me. Remember how much I love you. Remember what it felt like to believe that you could change the world, to believe that somehow, quietly, the world was already changing. And when you are feeling alone, when you need strength, when you feel as if you have lost the little direction or purpose you ever had, find your way back to the table."

He lifts the cup, gives thanks, and invites each of us to drink from it in turn. "This is the promise," he says, "that you will never be alone. This is the promise that you are loved beyond your wildest imagination. This is the promise that none of it—the believing, the hoping, the dreaming, the following—none of it has been in vain."

We began as strangers. We're not sure why we came. We're not sure of what comes next. Whatever it was that we came looking for, what we found was a table. A table where we all belong, despite our differences, despite our uncertainties, regardless of our misunderstandings. A table where we all belong, not because of anything we have done, not because of who we are or any fumbling answers we think we might have as to what this is all about, but because of who he is. The disciples didn't know this supper would be the last one. Let us hope, as we take our places here, that it is the first of many.

21 Witnessing a Miracle

A Bystander

I have thought about that day many times since it happened, yet it still surprises me how much I remember about it—hundreds and thousands of pesky little insignificant details. I suppose I have forgotten at least twice as many as I remember. I do know it was hot. It had not rained for quite a while, which made for dusty roads and blistered feet. It sounded like a riot or a party or some mixture of both, and even through the cloud of dust I could see the branches being pulled down from the trees and waved like mad and then thrown onto the ground. People were singing and holding their children up in the air and paving the road with their clothes. If it sounds strange the way I describe it, if it sounds unreal, then I'm doing a pretty good job. It *was* strange. Scary almost, the way people were laughing and dancing and shouting. I even found myself getting caught up in it, cheering for—what? I didn't know. It's intoxicating, you know, all those people. You figure they know what they're doing, they must—there's so many of them, you just join in. There was so much anticipation, so much hope. I fell into the same trap as all the others, imagining the puzzle piece that would fill up the hole inside me—imagining the answer I needed just walking down that narrow road.

When I finally saw what they—what *we*—had been waiting for, my heart broke. It broke in a place I had never felt before, a deep down kind of hurt that I have never felt since and I hope will never feel again. To see all those shouting people, dancing and singing as if they had found a treasure, like starving people at a feast, to get caught up in all their celebration and then to see what I saw . . . I guess I had more expectations than I realized, but I didn't know that until they were shattered by that wiry little man and his donkey.

I laughed out loud at first, thinking that this must be a joke, some cruel and ridiculous festival of the absurd, cheering for this fellow. Maybe someone was coming behind him. I could've picked better candidates for king out of that desperate, shouting crowd. But my laughter ended as abruptly as it began when I saw his face more closely. Even through the dust, I could see the tears, the shock. His eyes seemed to be watching something none of the rest of us could see, and I remember wondering why he didn't just turn the donkey around. I suppose it's good that he even had that animal, for I'm not sure he could've carried himself that day.

It turned out to be like all the other parades I've seen, a lot of foolish excitement about nothing real. I'm embarrassed to admit that I let myself get so captivated by all that, but there's this part of you deep down that wants so much to believe in something, to hope for something. I guess you never really gain control over that part of your heart—it just explodes in you at the strangest times, the most inopportune moments . . . I know I'm babbling, but I want you to see what I saw that day, to understand that even afterwards, even after I had seen him, there was still this little voice in me that wanted to keep screaming "Hosanna"—to keep dancing. Maybe it's impossible to explain. I heard later he turned out to be a criminal, and I guess I'm not surprised. At the very least, he was most certainly a con man, and for a moment that morning, I bought whatever it was that he was selling.

The Woman at Bethany

I am not an impulsive person by nature. I am not one of these peo-ple who can say what they mean all the time, or mean anything they say. To tell you the truth, I have always envied those around me who seem to so easily bare their soul and speak of their passion.

So how do I explain my actions? How do I tell you why I did what I did? I'm not even sure I know. Even now, so long after-wards, it seems more like a dream or a trance. I remember being so caught up with whatever it was that made me do it that even as I ran to the merchant's house, I felt like a visitor in someone else's body—like someone else was choosing my steps for me, telling me where to go, revealing to me what I had to do. It seems ridiculous now, so out of that moment, but it made perfect sense to me then. It seemed as if I had never had such a perfect idea, never needed to do something as much as I needed to do this thing. I ran like a nervous lover asking for the hand of his beloved in marriage, fool-ish and brilliant at the same time, desiring nothing more than to give my days away to the object of my devotion.

At first he didn't want to even sell it to me. He said it was too much, that I had been drinking, that I would regret it later. If I would just think about it, he said, cooler heads would prevail. But he finally gave in when he saw that I was not going to change my mind, and I watched as he took almost everything I had in exchange for the pound of sweet-smelling fragrance.

It must have been just a few minutes' walk to the house where the Nazarene was staying, but it felt like hours. I will not tell you that I didn't question my decision with every step, but somehow those voices of doubt seemed ridiculous to me at the time. The rea-sonable and rational thought that had been my companion for every one of my days seemed to be speaking a foreign language that day, or maybe it was me who spoke a new tongue—either way, the voices of caution and propriety were overwhelmed by the voice of my soul.

I was breathless by the time I arrived at the door, from alter-nately sprinting and walking my way down the road. When some-one finally opened the door, I'm not sure if I said anything or not, I just remember seeing his face almost immediately. I had seen it from a distance, but never so close. Even being so near, it felt as if he was miles away, like I could not ever be close enough to him. I would like to tell you now what he looked like, the way his eyes locked on you and drew you in, but it is not something to be held by words. Even memory does not suffice to tell it, but let me say that for that tiny minute, it was as if my heart had painted the world, as if my life held purpose, as if the universe were caught up in some cosmic drama, and the author of it all sat at a table before me.

I had not even thought of what to do with the gift I had brought him, but as I held it nervously in my hands, I felt my knees bend to the floor, and I pulled my hair out from under my shawl. To say then that I washed his feet seems to deny the moment of its beauty, of its mystery. We were the only two in the world, and at the same time, the entire world and all of life itself seemed to be wrapped up in that single moment. I didn't speak a word. Even now I don't know what I could've said, and as soon as it was over, I got up and walked out as they began to argue over what I had done.

I would love to tell you that ever since then I have been a different person, and in many countless ways, I suppose I have. But that voice has never returned. Sometimes I think I hear it, in the middle of the night or in the moments when I think of him, but my defenses are stronger these days, I guess, and it never takes hold of me like it did on that day. Some days I would give everything I have to hear that voice as clearly, and others I am desperately afraid of what it might make me do.

Judas

I'm not sure it's even worth speaking, as I am sure that you have already formed your judgments of my character, of my decisions. The human spirit wants more than anything to draw its lines between good and evil in thick clarity, to protect itself from the horror and emptiness of ambiguity. You need me to be the bad guy, because that makes it easier for you to pretend there is nothing in me that is also in you, none of my poison running through your veins, none of your humanness running through mine. It would even be easier for me to believe that I was simply evil or ignorant, that I possessed a kind of dark integrity that led me to the actions by which history has defined me. But that line, that thin space between right and wrong, is no boundary at all. It is where we live our lives. It is the sum of who we are, the air we breathe.

For I loved him as much as you. More, even. He was my friend, my teacher. No one listened as closely as I did, no one loved him more—not Peter, not James, not John, not you. And no one believed in his power more than I did—from the first time I saw him I knew what he could do for us—sometimes I think I saw more in him than he saw in himself. He was so reluctant to be the Messiah, so reluctant to show his power, to end the suffering of our people—but I knew all along it was in him. The thing I couldn't understand is why he waited, why he put up with so much, why he took everything so slow. He came so close so many times, turning over the tables of the moneychangers, talking about the new king-dom that was coming—in the back of my mind I thought, he just needs a push. He needs a reason to fight. All these others need to see what I have seen, what he's capable of.

I smiled as I kissed him, imagining the spectacle I was about to witness, thinking in the back of my mind the important part I was playing in changing the world. In my mind I saw the skies tearing open and the face of God revealing itself to those soldiers and to all of us and . . . But it was not to be. None of it. One of the oth-ers drew his sword and swung at the ear of a guard, but that is all. There was no fight. There was no change. And in that moment, I died. Long before the scratchy rope tightened around my neck, I gave up on my life. Maybe no one in history has ever been as wrong. Maybe no one has ever been as right. Go on believing whatever it is that helps you to sleep at night. Go on thinking I am different than you, that you would have expected less of him. What I *can* tell you is that no one can live very long without a heart. And in that dark garden, mine was taken from me, hauled away in shackles.

Jesus

To be human is to be afraid, I suppose. We spend so much of our lives being afraid of the stuff that hurts us. Our doubt, our pain—the very idea of dying seems to frighten us out of our skin. I guess I came out here because I am afraid of that, too. I do love this life—I love the sound of laughter, and the way tears feel in your eyes just before they stream down your cheek. The sound of wood shavings crackling beneath my sandal. That child's face in Capernaum. The breeze off the water. The way my mother says my name. I love so many things I never thought I would—I keep telling myself I have prepared to lose all the big things, to make these sacrifices to stay on the path, but it is the million little things I am most afraid of losing. I keep wanting to imagine that I am so different from all of them, all those faces in the crowd with their frightened eyes and their desperation, but I really am just like them. Just to feel this fear inside me, it is so powerful, it makes you feel so distant, I can't imagine death feeling any worse than this.

I know you're not in the habit of answering questions, but I wish you would say something. I guess I've taken for granted all the other times, but I need a word from you tonight. Anything would be okay. I need to know if this is the way, if this is where you want me, where you're calling me. I need to know if you're even still there. Even my prayers feel lonely lately. It seems as if I am surrounded by everyone in the world, but there are none whom I can talk to, no one who can listen to what I must say. When I close my eyes to try and pray, I see everything I might lose—don't you need me here, to heal and to teach and to feed? I could do so much more with just a bit more time. I feel each minute now as they slip by. I know it must be close, and I worry that I won't be ready, that I won't know what to do . . . Please say something.

Maybe I already know what you would say. This cup is mine to drink. It always has been, I know that now. These days of darkness are part of the sweetness of all the rest. I know that, I do.

Watch over all of the others, they have no idea what's coming, as many times as I've tried to tell them. Their hearts weren't ready to hear it then, and I'm afraid they'll be even less ready for it now. I just wish they could . . .

I hear them. They're coming up the hill. My hour has come. Be with me now. Be with me. AMEN.

The Centurion

Your skin gets thick pretty quickly. I got sick almost every day in the beginning, just the sight of death over and over and over again. I guess it was too much. I don't know what changed, I suppose I just got used to it. Numbness has its place. I know that sounds cold, but you just have to protect yourself from all of it. Shut it out and do your job. Not that it ever gets easy, some of them scream so loud, especially when the nails go in. In my night-mares I always hear those screams, them begging for mercy, saying they're sorry and they'll never do it again. Some of them are so young, too, not even as old as me, and you just want to look the other way, but somebody's got to do it, you know? It's not like I made any of the decisions to kill any of them—but I never see Pilate or any of the others at one of these executions. I wonder if they would think twice if they knew what kind of death they were sending these men to—what kind of life they had indirectly sen-tenced *us* to . . .

I remember this one in particular. I try and forget their faces, but this one I can see as clearly as I see yours. They had already beaten him up pretty bad by the time he got here, and there was a group of soldiers and peasants around him giving him a hard time, kicking at him and spitting. That's not unusual when the crime is really horrible, so I assumed this was a murderer or some-thing, the way they were getting so angry. I guess I just assumed they knew what they were doing, because I got caught up in it, too, and before I knew it I was taking my turn pushing him around and screaming insults in his ear. I'm horrified now just to remember it, I mean, I didn't even know the man, I just assumed that . . . since the others . . .

He didn't scream, just a little grunt when we pinned him. And he didn't say much before he died, he just shouted out in one of the Jewish languages. I couldn't understand what he said, but I knew he wasn't talking to any of us that were there. It made those women cry even louder, I can't even talk about that—they were so . . . sad. I'd never seen a murderer with so many mourners around, if I had just put two and two together . . .

He died about three in the afternoon, I think. It seemed like midnight, it was so dark. He just gave out this loud groan, and seized up, and it was over. Just another one dead before his time, another son or brother or husband lost. But this one was different. I am not educated or religious or anything like that, but I know this one was different. I felt it in the pit of my stomach, in the depth of my heart. This one was different.

I don't know where the words came from—when they came out of my mouth they were as new to me as they were to those around me, but I knew they were true. "Truly, this man was the Son of God." The others wrote it off as a nervous fit, but it didn't go away. The more I said the words over and over again in my head, the more I knew that they were the truest thing I'd ever known.

At the end of that day, I walked away from that place, and I have never returned. I didn't know where to go, I just know I had to leave. And I am still walking away, still trying to understand, still staring at those same eyes when I fall asleep at night. Whatever it means, he was it, you know. *He was it.*

22 Easter: Breaking Free

On the other side of death.
Expecting the familiar smells of ending,
*   the pain of goodbye*
*   the cracked mirror of mortality*
*   our hearts fumbling to fill the empty space.*
But then
*   everything has changed*
*   or maybe nothing has changed*
*   and we see it clearly now*
for the first time
through his eyes.

It is death that is empty.

On the other side of death
*   . . . is Life.*

I hope the words finally sunk in this Easter.

Because all the while we've been inside our sanctuaries, calmly singing "Christ is risen," there have been women running breathlessly up and down the streets saying the same thing to themselves, but with a panicked tone, not sure if there should be an exclamation point or a question mark at the end of their sentence. He is risen! He is risen? Meanwhile the disciples have been huddling together in fear and brokenheartedness, thinking the women's madness is nothing more than an "idle tale," Luke tells us.

The truth of the matter is, whenever new life breaks in, something usually has to break to make room for it. A risen Savior is not something you can just set out an extra plate for and be done with. New life changes everything. It pulls the rug out from underneath us, then the floor out from underneath the rug. So before we sing another song and get ourselves all comfortable with this whole "Jesus is alive" thing, I want us to really understand what we're signing up for here.

The first two weeks my first child was home, I got up at least eight times a night to put my ear against his face, to check and make sure he was still breathing. Or I'd get up and recheck the way I'd folded his blanket, positive that I had done it wrong and he was therefore not going to develop normally. People can talk forever about how your life will change once a child comes into it, but they might as well be speaking Portuguese. There are simply not words. New life means that there is no room for old life. He is risen! He is risen?

It is unbelievable. It is chaotic. It is a blessing, the best blessing of all, but it fits into the old patterns of life about as well as an attention-deficit, hammer-wielding eight-year-old fits into a china shop. Things can't stay the same. And sometimes that hurts a lot.

It is hard to deal with Easter. God won't stay where we put him. He won't hide. He won't stay still. We wrap him up in death linens and he makes a rainbow. We put him on a cross and he whispers, "Forgive them." We try and wrap our heads around what he might do next and he slips out the back door on his way down a new road.

New life is awkward and tough and heartbreaking. But I tell you what—it is also a promise—that every suffering can lead to hope, every tear of sadness can be traded in for a tear of heartbursting wonder, that every dark Friday leads to a bright, unexpected Sunday.

I hope the words sunk in this Easter. I hope you heard them. I hope you felt them. Because whether or not you're ready for it, life is outside the door, just waiting to take you and me down a new road. My prayer is that the ends of all our divergent and winding paths are the same. Otherwise this is just another idle tale. But my suspicion is that it is much more than that.

23 The God Who Won't Stay Put

Jesus said to her, "Woman, why are you weeping? Whom are you looking for?" Supposing him to be the gardener, she said to him, "Sir, if you have carried him away, tell me where you have laid him, and I will take him away." Jesus said to her, "Mary!" She turned and said to him in Hebrew, "Rabbouni!" (which means Teacher). Jesus said to her, "Do not hold on to me, because I have not yet ascended to the Father. But go to my brothers and say to them, 'I am ascending to my Father and your Father, to my God and your God.'" Mary Magdalene went and announced to the disciples, "I have seen the Lord"; and she told them that he had said these things to her. (John 20:15–18)

If he had just stayed where we put him, things would have been easier. If he had stayed in the manger with the cattle and the sheep and the dirt and smell and his nobody parents, things would have been easier. If he had not set down his chisel and hammer and walked out of that carpenter's workshop after so many years of living a decent and respectable and normal existence, things would have been easier. If he had held his truth inside him like the rest of us, things would have been easier. If he had let the hurt go on hurting, abandoned the abandoned, forgotten all the forgotten, things would have been easier. He really should have stayed quiet.

99

He really should have been content to live the life assigned to him, quiet and unnoticed, in the shadows. If he had done that, this past Friday would have never—well, you know. Things would have been easier. But that is not something he seemed to understand.

He must have known they would kill him, building up the people's hopes until they were shouting "king" and "son of David" at him in broad daylight. And then to see him just sitting there, not doing a thing, not leading a revolution or organizing the people, of course they had to kill him. That is what you do to someone who breaks your heart like that. They had so little to hope for, they put so much faith in him, he seemed to return so little. He didn't even die well. He just died. And it seems that this story ends just like the others. Sure—it shone a little brighter, it carried us a little further, maybe we will remember it longer, but it ended just like the rest. He just died. If he had just stayed where we put him, things would have been easier.

And now, we stare down into the depths of a tomb. It reeks of death and funeral homes and old hymns on pipe organs and uncomfortable formality—all the things we are most afraid of. The walk up here was so quiet. It seems that the moments when there is the most that needs to be said, the greatest need to question and understand, we are the most ill-equipped to speak. We got up and dressed this morning, wanting to pay our respects, to leave a few flowers, to do something—*anything*, after pretending all weekend that we weren't thinking about it, that we weren't thinking about him. And so we walked together in silence, remembering to ourselves the strangeness of the paths he had led us on. Until we saw Mary.

You could barely make out any of the words she was saying, but it was clear that something was wrong. And so we ran until we were out of breath. Thinking foolishly that there might be something we could do—we have been given so many chances to do something and never taken them, but for some reason, we ran this time. And as our eyes adjusted to the darkness, we saw exactly what Mary had seen—absolutely nothing. The body is missing. And all that is inside us—the stored up grief, all those tears we could not shed, all the words we could not say—all of it explodes—not into sadness, but into anger. Who could have done such a thing? We sit there for a few moments, again, in silence, but there is nothing we can do, no one we can go to, he is not there to tell us what to think or where to go, he is just not there. And so that's where we would rather be. Anywhere but there.

But Mary stays. We couldn't talk her into leaving if we tried—she doesn't seem to even hear us. She has no other place to go, or she thinks that if she looks hard enough his body will appear again in the shadows, or maybe something deep inside her soul knows something she's not aware of yet. For whatever reason, she stays, weeping, which is a polite way of saying that she completely loses it. Chest-heaving, breath-stopping, crying out, bawling. The crying she could not do before. They could take his life, steal his body, but her grief—no one could take that away. At least that is what she thought.

Because she is not alone. She does not hear them walk up, she does not recognize their faces but somehow recognizes them all the same. Where she was alone before, there are now two strangers. Angels, the Gospel writer says, but for Mary, they were just strangers. "Woman, why are you weeping?" It seems that it is always the worst moments when strangers want to introduce themselves to you. You are in Wal-Mart or the grocery store or sitting down by yourself in the cafeteria and they find you. "Is everything okay?" And you want to say, "It was until you came along can't you see that I just want to be alone in my misery and I don't even know who you are can I please just have some space!" but you manage to stifle it into "I'm fine, thanks." Mary can't even do that, though. Because by the time she has turned around to say something, she runs smack into a third stranger, who smells even more familiar, looks even more like a friend, whose eyes seem as if they know her well. And of course, they do—they are the eyes that know all of us, call each of us without a sound—they are *his* eyes. And there, in that moment, hearing her own name again, this woman who was looking for a dead corpse finds a living miracle. A kept promise. The gospel itself.

And his words to her are important for us to hear: *"Don't hold on to me. It's not all finished, you know. I am on my way, and you have to let me go."* Not that she was holding on to him with her hands, she was as unable to do that as we are now—instead she was looking at him, hoping in her heart of hearts that this meant he was coming back. That he was on his way to the disciples and the old neighborhood and the way things were. "Don't hold on to me," he said, and he could have just as easily said, *"I'm not going that way. I'm on my way to God. And I'm taking the whole world with me."*

It doesn't so much matter that Jesus died for you. All that proves is that death and pain and sorrow are real and powerful. We already knew that much. The kind of Friday faith that comes with Jesus' death lets us off the hook, because it keeps the ball in God's court. It doesn't matter so much that he died for you, because the real miracle is that he lives for you. We are who we are not because Christ died for us, but because Christ lives for us. And that means something. It is more than historical fact—if the truth of the resurrection is merely that God resuscitates a body, then it is not worth our lives. But the truth of the resurrection is something that is not only true in one moment, but true in all moments. Things have changed. We should have known it all along—the baby in the cattle stall, the pitiful little branch sprouting in the middle of the desert, the candle in the overwhelming darkness—they all hinted at what was coming. Life out of death, light out of darkness, resurrection out of a cross.

So bring your doubts. Bring your pain. Bring your uncertainty. Whether or not we believe it, whether or not we are ready to receive it, God is alive. That is what has called us here, that is what makes us get up out of bed every reluctant morning, that is what finally gives us eyes to see the impossible. To see life, with all its rough edges and open wounds, coming toward us. In the most frightening and exciting sense of the word, the resurrection is true. For all of us. God breaks free. That is the end, the beginning, and the middle of all our stories. *God breaks free.* Love will find its own direction. We cannot push that love away, no matter how determined our efforts, no matter how firmly entrenched in our sadness we may be—nothing can hold it back now. Nothing. So don't hold on to him. As much as we would rather do that, keeping him in a box and deciding when to let him out, when to listen, it is his turn to hold on to us. To take us into the impossible, the unseen, the unpredictable. Things would have been easier if he had just stayed where we put him. But then, that wouldn't be like him, would it?

24 Whispering Nonsense

When the sabbath was over, Mary Magdalene, and Mary the mother of James, and Salome bought spices, so that they might go and anoint him. And very early on the first day of the week, when the sun had risen, they went to the tomb. They had been saying to one another, "Who will roll away the stone for us from the entrance to the tomb?" When they looked up, they saw that the stone, which was very large, had already been rolled back. As they entered the tomb, they saw a young man, dressed in a white robe, sitting on the right side; and they were alarmed. But he said to them, "Do not be alarmed; you are looking for Jesus of Nazareth, who was crucified. He has been raised; he is not here. Look, there is the place they laid him. But go, tell his disciples and Peter that he is going ahead of you to Galilee; there you will see him, just as he told you." So they went out and fled from the tomb, for terror and amazement had seized them; and they said nothing to anyone, for they were afraid. (Mark 16:1–8)

H*e is not here. He is risen.*

If you're like me, those words stand the hairs up on the back of your neck, even though you've heard them a million times.

What we forget is that when we hear them now, we hear them across thousands of years, millions of pages of interpretation and analysis, billions of wordy sermons and countless old hymns. They're easier to shout when you've got that kind of distance between you and the resurrection. We're safe here, at this distance, more like sixth graders staring at a textbook than people discovering the story for the first time because it's their lives and it's not so scripted, not so predictable. But I'm not sure we can even understand the words unless we hear them from the other side of the page, hearing them not as a shout, but as a whisper.

I suppose that you'll need to paint the scene with your own images, your own memories, because we all have been there at one point or another, but I imagine it looked different to each one of us. Some of you will see twisted steel and broken glass, bent guardrails and flashing red lights, the smell of spilt gasoline and exploding airbags, the awe of stunned onlookers slowing to see the carnage, wondering how many have been lost, the hurried phone calls to say that something has happened and that you have to come now. Because it is so sudden, we have no time to prepare, there seems to be no logic here, just the physics of destruction and collision, the broken hearts of unexplainable tragedy. I imagine for some of us this is what it will look like.

For others it will be the face of a loved one, distorted and swollen from the chemotherapy, bald from the radiation. The machines with their beeping and ticking and blinking, tied like puppet strings to veins and ventilators, keeping them alive but not alive as they were before, not dead but not the same person, so that we do not know whether to mourn their dying or weep for their living. It is the ten-year-old boy who is suddenly scared of his grandfather because he has never seen suffering like that, and he touches his hand because his mother tells him to, but this is certainly not the man who showed him how to use stilts in the backyard, whose laugh shook the house. It is the faces of those still in the waiting room, who are as sick as those they are praying for, only in a different more incurable kind of way, as they leaf blankly through the expired magazine for the zillionth time.

It is the distant memory that seems so far away most of the time and shouldn't bother us anymore, but then we expect to see her car and we remember we'll never see her car again, or we set out dinner for eight and remember there are only seven of us now, how could we forget, we know better, and we are angry that it still has so much power over us, creeping up on us and disrupting the little charade of normalcy we had begun to accept as reality.

Others will peer through the television screen to see the broken bodies of a mother and her unborn son, carried away from the water in plastic bags, victims of some evil that is too unspeakable to name, but looks so much like us we cannot stop our watching. Or we will change the channel to find the family that has lost their only child to drugs or war or gang violence, and for a moment we sense their deep pain, but only for that small moment, before we decide we don't need to get caught up in all that, it is too far away from us, too removed from our cozy and sheltered lives. We choose when and where we want to feel with the remote control, turning it off when we have had enough. But in the frightening times, when the stories leap out of that little box and into our own lives, when we are awakened in the middle of the night with irrational fear or we are driving and suddenly we don't know what we're to do with ourselves, we realize it is not so far away, not so different.

There are other examples, of course, and I know that you have to find your own. For the sake of our story, I invite you to one in particular, long ago but not so different from these that we have named. It is a lonely tomb on the outskirts of town. It is three women on a road, waking before dawn to make this pilgrimage. It is their memory of his dying, his crying out, his bleeding and suffocation and pain and ugliness up there on that cross, the removing of the nails and the dragging of his lifeless body from that horrible hill. It is the sight of his face without life, the empty eyes that once were full beyond measure, alive beyond anything an artist could have painted or a dreamer could have imagined. It is this road that they walk toward his burial place.

It is the small talk they keep as they walk, speaking not of their fear, not of their loss, not of the heaviness of their hearts, but of the little things that always surround funerals, the petty details that keep the heart on safe ground, like meal planning and guest lists and who will roll away the stone door. You walk for the same reason you are talking about such trivial things, for to stop and stand in the silence is to let it all catch up with you, which you know in your rational mind will happen at any moment, but you keep going in the hopes that it will lose your trail, that it will forget about you and leave you alone.

They have brought spices, and they fidget with them in their nervous hands as they walk, grateful to fill the lulls of silence with talk about the sweet fragrance, the kindness of the storeowner and the rumored marriage of his daughter, only to hit another stand-still and just hear the sounds of their sandals on the loose gravel and dirt. Their eyes look like blank pages, that kind of empty tearlessness that only comes when you have cried every tear you had in you, and you come to the sorrow that is beyond anything describable in words.

And it seems like hours and hours have passed before they finally reach their destination, but it has of course only been a brief journey. They take one deep breath together, look at each other, and begin to climb the short hill. But when they get there, when they make it to the door, well, you know already. Nothing's as it should be. Nothing's in place. The stone has been rolled away. There is no body but that of a stranger who whispers nonsense about Jesus doing this and that and headed off to Galilee as if this were just a normal day, as if dead bodies walked around all the time. And this is where I need you to stay with me, because I know that you already know—I know you have had the story well rehearsed for some time, you can almost recite the actors' lines and hum the closing music as the credits roll—but I need you to stay here.

I need you to keep the memories of your own walk to the tomb that we began with, the faces of those you love, the stiffness of the funeral ceremony, the awkward grief of the hospital bed—because it is only in staying in that place, your own source of pain and mourning and loss, that you will understand what happens next. Because when you know deeply that hurt, the words of resurrection mix with your grief like oil and water. There is no space. There is no way.

And so the women, who seemed to have nothing left in them, drop their spices, scream in fear and misunderstanding, and run like hell for who knows where. They certainly don't know where they're going, they just know they cannot stay here. There are no congratulatory handshakes, no trumpets, no Easter lilies. They speak to no one, for what would they say? What would they tell?

Those of us with the benefit of the script, knowing what we know, we can sit here from this distance and recite creeds and sing our Easter songs and delight all we want to in this first resurrection. But I think the truth of it is that we cannot know the sweetness of Easter until we live through the pain of our own Good Fridays, which don't seem very good at all and don't end on Friday. We cannot begin to live into the celebration of Easter, the promise of radical love that cannot be held down, until we feel the desperate need for that love, the pit in our stomachs and the lump in our throats and the nauseating sadness that tells us we are human and that we are alive, though we may not want to be either just now.

And we probably need to hear this, because I don't want to be mistaken—it doesn't mean that death and fear and darkness are all null and void now, no matter how much we'd like to pretend that is the case. It doesn't mean we should ignore our pain and smile for the camera and talk ourselves into happiness because that's what good Christians do. No. Death still comes, and death still hurts. We hang the cross in the middle of our sanctuaries and around our necks to remind us of that. To remind us that it was real. That his screams and his death and his fear were real. That our tears are real. That our grief is real. That cancer and car wrecks and murder and divorce and all the rest of it are real. But so is God.

The message of Easter Sunday is not that God will take away all our worries. God is not in that business. And I've come to believe that the message is not that God sends his Son to be killed because that's what the world really needs. The message of Easter Sunday is that come what may, whatever tomb we find ourselves in, if we look close enough, we will see the footprints of God who has been there, too. Whatever hurt we are trapped in, we will never ever ever ever be alone.

And as we stand here at the door of this tomb, watching the women run away, we have to choose what our response will be. I imagine that not many of us will run from this place. We are too well conditioned, too safe right now. But I do invite you to wander away from this place in the spirit of resurrection, in the power and promise of confusion, in the grace of unexpected change. And in those days to come or those days that you're in, when you make your way to the tomb to pay your respects, to sign the guest book and offer your prayers, dressed in black and wondering what to say to the family, don't be surprised if things don't turn out the way you expected them to. Because he is not here. He is risen. And whatever that means, whatever it doesn't mean, it is the truest thing ever whispered.

25 When the Resurrection Finds You

When it was evening on that day, the first day of the week, and the doors of the house where the disciples had met were locked for fear of the Jews, Jesus came and stood among them and said, "Peace be with you." After he said this, he showed them his hands and his side. Then the disciples rejoiced when they saw the Lord. Jesus said to them again, "Peace be with you. As the Father has sent me, so I send you." When he had said this, he breathed on them and said to them, "Receive the Holy Spirit. If you forgive the sins of any, they are forgiven them; if you retain the sins of any, they are retained." But Thomas (who was called the Twin), one of the twelve, was not with them when Jesus came. So the other disciples told him, "We have seen the Lord." But he said to them, "Unless I see the mark of the nails in his hands, and put my finger in the mark of the nails and my hand in his side, I will not believe." A week later his disciples were again in the house, and Thomas was with them. Although the doors were shut, Jesus came and stood among them and said, "Peace be with you." Then he said to Thomas, "Put your finger here and see my hands. Reach out your hand and put it in my side. Do not doubt but believe." Thomas answered him, "My Lord and my God!" Jesus said to him, "Have you believed because you have seen me? Blessed are those who have not seen and yet have come to believe." (John 20:19–29)

It is one thing to find the resurrection. It is quite another thing altogether to have the resurrection come and find you. It is one thing for those women who were wandering down the road toward a tomb to find it empty, to find an angel who looks more like a stranger saying "he's not here, go to Galilee, he's on his way there, if you hurry you can beat him" and all sorts of other bizarre nonsense. It is quite another thing altogether to be in the privacy of your own hiding place, huddled with nine or so of your closest clueless associates behind locked doors and shuttered windows, and have him show up, without the courtesy of knocking or at the very least a *"Honey, I'm home. . . ."*

Now I understand if you feel as if this is overdoing it. After all, it's been two thousand years. Easter was just last week, and Jesus having already been resurrected for us, well, it just seems a bit blasé, all this appearing again and again. For heaven's sake, we get the point. We got all dressed up last week, we brought our Easter lilies, we woke up the whole family to come and see the empty tomb, even Uncle Charles, who we all know only gives up his Sunday fishing trip on a rare occasion. We would rather be getting back to our normal schedule here, we just can't have Jesus going and being resurrected every Sunday now, can we? It's just not practical. There are musicians to hire and chairs to set out and family suppers to cook and new dresses to buy, it takes so much time and money these days to pull off a good Easter Sunday, we just don't have it in us to do this every week.

And I can assure you that no one would agree with you more than these disciples, whom we find this morning crowded into a dark room looking more like an oversized broom closet than a hiding place. It is one thing to blow trumpets and give each other high-fives and throw confetti and understand what the heck is going on that first Easter Sunday, and the disciples are not quite ready to do any of those things just yet. In fact, to be brutally honest, they are nowhere near ready to do any of that, because for them the resurrection is not yet a party, it is only a rumor.

They have been around Jesus long enough to know that you do not take things at face value, and anyway, there is not a lot of established prerogative for dead people getting up and leaving their resting places. There is no manual for how to be a disciple under such conditions. And sure, those of us with the faith of hindsight can sit here with two thousand years of perspective under our belts and say, "well, he did warn them," but I imagine we would be just as frightened if Jesus walked in here this morning, if we even noticed. So they do what any of us do when we are faced with the death of a loved one: they try to eat something though no one is hungry, they tell each other everything will be just fine though no one in the room is sure of that anymore, and they talk about the little things though every heart in there has come face to face with a brokenness and a despair too deep to measure.

Because while you have been at work or at school or at home or playing golf or eating with friends these past few days, they have been cramped up here. And while each of us have had Easter written on our calendars and Palm Pilots for months now so that we could plan ahead and thaw out the turkey in time, nothing runs as smoothly the first time through. So instead of hunting for Easter eggs or listening to the choir, they are hiding from the authorities, hiding from the memory of his death, hiding from the hurt. Well, maybe they're not so different from us.

One of the things that's not so different between them and us is that they have the same little voice in the back of their minds that hopes he will show up. You know the one. You've had it since Sunday school the first time, when you didn't know any better and you thought Jesus might just walk right in one morning to answer your questions or heal your sick friend. And as much as you'd like to pretend that you've grown out of that phase, that your faith has matured thanks to years of theological inquiry and scriptural analysis, the child in you, the one who doesn't know any better, is still waiting for him to walk through that door. In some ways, I guess we're not so different at all from these frightened friends two thousand years our seniors, because they didn't think it would happen either.

And what I'm referring to, of course, is his showing up the way he did. There are ten in the room one minute, and then without warning there are eleven. He whispers to them, "Peace be with you," which has, like most of his instructions to the disciples, the opposite effect. And they do their best to disappear in that tiny room, but you know as well as I do that there is no hiding from him once he comes looking for you. But they try all the same, climbing over one another screaming and carrying on and trying to make themselves invisible underneath the table.

But after a short while that feels more like a few short years, they stop gritting their teeth and one by one they open their eyes to see the face of their dinner guest. And they discover what you and I already know, that it's *him*, though that makes as little sense to them as it might to us. To show them finally that he is who he says he is, that he is the same one that they left their fishing boats and tax collector booths and families and all things familiar for, he shows them the holes in his body. Now we can wonder all day long why he does this or what it means, but suffice it to say that for these ten friends it means that this is no angel, this is no random apparition, but this is their teacher, the same one who broke bread with them just days ago, the same one who was killed as they began their hiding. Not that they wouldn't have trusted an angel or a Jesus without the wounds, but somehow it is his pain, his suffering, that lets them know this is the one they've been waiting for. And suddenly they know it's true.

And knowing that maybe now they'll be able to hear it, he whispers again, "Peace be with you." And they crowd in on him with all the tears and surprise of a reunion, the kind that comes when lovers reconcile after a fight or you see your best friend in the supermarket after fifteen years or the test results come back and you have more time than you thought you did—a reunion like that, multiplied exponentially. The story says they get close enough to him to feel his breath, which we can certainly understand, since they have felt so distant from him in their fear and cowardice. "Receive the Spirit," he says, already knowing that what they need most now is the same as what we would need thousands of years later, a friend in all this, a companion on the journey. And then, as if he's picking up a conversation he started with them long ago, "If you forgive the sins of any, they are forgiven; if you remember them, they are remembered against them." And then as quickly as he showed up, he is gone again. And that is the end of a very good story.

But it is not, as you know, the whole story. Because one is missing. We don't know where he is, your guess is as good as mine. For whatever reason, he chose not to be hiding in the room with his friends. Maybe he went home to his family, maybe he was wandering down the streets of Galilee, needing a breath of fresh air and a clear moment to think about all that had happened. He couldn't have known, as we never know, that his choice not to be in that room would leave a permanent mark in history, and that we would all be introduced to him not as Thomas, the pioneer of the faith in the land called India, or Thomas, the disciple who, wanting to keep himself close to Jesus at all costs, had asked him earlier, "How can we know the way?" Instead, we all meet Doubting Thomas, Thomas of little faith. All for being in the wrong place at the wrong time.

So when he does find the others, and they are interrupting each other in their excitement, cutting off each other's sentences to tell him what has happened, it may be hard to understand his reaction. Those of us who have been so conditioned to belief without sight tend to feel threatened by those who are willing to ask the tough questions. Rather than talk about the places the Bible makes no sense, let's just have another prayer. Rather than talking about where the church has failed to live up to its purpose in the world, let's sing another song. Rather than truly try to love another through the broken and sticky awkwardness of human compassion and relationship, let's form a committee to look into that. And we tell each other that this is no place for questions, no place for hurt, no place for doubt. This is not a place to struggle, because in your wrestling you might shatter the thin walls that we have each built to protect ourselves from the unanswered questions—*Why did she have to die so early? Why did he fall out of love with me? Who could do such a thing?* Those are not questions for church—those are questions for the middle of the sleepless night, not for the polished veneer of Sunday morning.

So it may anger some of you when Thomas says what he says. I warn you because it's not the kind of thing any of us want to hear. "Unless I see with my own eyes where the nails went in, unless I jab my finger into the hole in his side, I don't want to hear any more of this."

Now I would like to end this here and tell you, poor Thomas, if he had only tried a bit harder, if he had read his devotional book a few more times, if he had just prayed about it, he would have known better—don't make the same mistake, enjoy your lunch and go in peace.

But you see, Thomas's doubt is not the enemy of faith. Thomas's questions do not stand in the way of his believing, they are the path *to* his believing. Thomas does not say that he wants to touch the wounds of his master out of irreverence or apathy, he speaks those words out of his deep longing for Jesus. His deep love for his one true Lord. Out of memory for his beloved friend and teacher, out of respect for the horrible death he was made to suffer alone.

And I should tell you, Jesus does come back for Thomas. About a week later, in the same locked-up room, Jesus shows up with a message for his old friend. And while Jesus gives Thomas the chance to touch his wounds, Thomas thinks better of it. Not because he is afraid, not because he's embarrassed, but suddenly, in that moment, he doesn't need to anymore. And it is Thomas—poor, doubting, faithless Thomas—who is the first one to declare that not only is this their risen Lord, but that he is looking at God himself. There is no other disciple who could make that claim, because it could only be made after a long journey of doubt and struggle.

And in a last touch of irony, as if to speak directly to all of us on the other side of these pages, Jesus does what he often does, declaring happy and blessed those who can count their blessings on their pinky finger. Jesus offers one more Beatitude, saying a little prayer for all of us who will be asked to believe without ever seeing a thing.

To find Christ is to find Christ with all his wounds, with all the baggage of hell on earth itself. To be found by Christ is to be found in a world broken by too many forces to count, many of them that look far too much like us. No matter our theological defenses, God will find us right where we are, just the way we are. Because faith is not just for those of us who can keep our heads above water, or keep our questions at bay—to be faithful is to be fearful, to feel the wounds of the world, to yell back at God in disbelief, to weep in misunderstanding. Because as Desmond Tutu and Martin Luther King Jr. and others have been telling us for so long, the opposite of faith is not doubt, it is indifference. To care for this story, to love God, is to struggle with everything you hold most dear.

The leap of faith is being able to hold your breath, cast your caution into the wind—to reach out into that world, to find your place in that world, to see through the hurt and doubt and uncertainty, and to find a Christ. To be huddled in the room of our own loneliness and uncertainty, only to find that there is no place we can go that God can't find us.

The best advice I can give you is a little dated, but I think it still packs some meaning for all of us on the journey—Peace be with you. Even when it seems that there is nothing left, *peace be with you*.

26 Knowing the Road by Heart

Now on that same day two of them were going to a village called Emmaus, about seven miles from Jerusalem, and talking with each other about all these things that had happened. While they were talking and discussing, Jesus himself came near and went with them, but their eyes were kept from recognizing him. (Luke 24:13–16)

One of the wonderful things about growing up in Alabama was that my entire family—my grandparents, my cousins and aunts and uncles—lived somewhere within the state. In fact, my nuclear family is the only one that ever really moved, so I have become very accustomed to my relatives' homes; they all live in the same houses they always have.

I have a lot of family that lives near Selma, and as a little kid, I had memorized all the houses and churches and road signs that marked the way to my grandparents' house down there. It's almost a two-hour drive, but I probably could have given you directions when I was four years old on exactly how to get there, because it was such an important road for me.

As we passed all those mile markers, I knew that every one that flashed by meant I was getting closer and closer to someone very important, and my heart became a kind of radar for sensing exactly how far we had left to go. For those of you who have never been to Selma, there is not much there to see these days. I think any casual visitor might become pretty bored. The scenery is not nearly as beautiful as it is in the northern part of the state or, for that matter, any other part of the state. The roads are fairly straight and level, the landscape is mountain-less and drab. There is just not much to look at.

Unless you are a kid on the way to his grandmother's house. Then everything changes. There are some streetlights that line the entrance into Selma proper, and as a kid I was convinced that they were put there for me, to tell me that I had finally made it to where I was going. I saw things differently on that road because I knew it by heart.

All of us have roads that mean something to us. Streets and highways that we know like the backs of our hands, either because they lead us to something important or because we have driven them so many times on the way to work or school or home that we have memorized every little detail—every curve, every pothole, every bright yellow sign.

They tell us these days that almost nine out of ten car wrecks happen within a mile of home for most people, on those stretches of familiar road. As I was thinking about that recently, it struck me that the reason that happens is that people are so comfortable with the roads near their house, they think they hold no more surprises for them. We know what to expect from the roads we know best.

At least that's what Cleopas and his friend thought as they made their way down the highway to Emmaus. I can almost guarantee you that this was not the first time they had walked that stretch of road. The scriptures tell us it was about a seven-mile walk from Jerusalem to Emmaus—short enough that you could walk it in just a few hours, and short enough that if you walked it enough times, you could really learn all there was to learn about it—every bump in the road, every sharp stone that might cut through your sandal, and every good watering stop.

Since they knew it so well, it was the perfect road to walk along and talk at the same time. Many a great conversation occurred along that stretch of land, as people walked alongside each other, sharing ideas and stories.

And the two who were walking this particular day were a lot like that, talking and sharing as they walked together. The biggest difference between this day and all the other times they had walked the path together was that the conversation was so unusual. It was Easter Sunday, but they didn't know that yet, because it was the very first Easter Sunday, and a lot had happened that day that they knew only bits and pieces about. It was so much food for thought they couldn't help discussing it as they traveled, but it didn't help their spirits very much.

Now I know that sounds strange, for people to be very sad on Easter, but we have to remember that for all Jesus' followers who didn't know yet about his resurrection, this was a Sunday like any other Sunday, except that they no longer had Jesus around. It had only been a few days since Jesus had been taken from them, arrested and crucified like a common criminal outside the gates of Jerusalem. It takes quite a while before you feel much like laughing or doing anything really after such a loss. It is only after a few days that you really start to grieve and mourn for the one you have lost.

And if that isn't enough to deal with, some of the women had spread rumors that his body was missing from the tomb. It seemed that they were doomed to lose him twice, even as people began to also say that he might be alive again. That seemed impossible—too much to hope for—it almost made it hurt worse to think such things. So for these two followers of Jesus, as they walked this road they had walked so many times before, it was not a particularly happy day.

Since he had died, they had spent their time hiding, afraid of what the authorities might do to them next. This was really the first time they had been able to talk freely about what had happened, and it makes sense that they were disappointed, not just because of the tremendous loss of their friend and teacher, but also because they felt they had lost their purpose.

Many of them had given their lives over to following this man and listening to everything he had to say, believing that he was the Messiah, the Chosen One of God. And they believed it with all their hearts, right up until the moment he died. Some of them even thought he might come down from the cross, or lead a great army at the last minute to save himself and all his followers, but of course, he didn't. He didn't do any of the things they imagined he might do. Of course, we know from the scriptures that he had told them many times that he had to die and rise again, but that is hard news to listen to. They wanted to hear different things—they had had enough death and grief and loss—they wanted Jesus to talk about life. They couldn't have imagined that all his talk about death was the truest talk about life any of them had ever heard.

So as these two made their way closer and closer to Emmaus, they spoke for the first time about their surprise and disappointment. They tried to talk about other things at first, but his name just kept coming up. Whenever you lose someone that important to you, it seems that while your sadness is the last thing you want to talk about, every conversation leads right back to it.

As they talked, they shared with each other the stories they remembered best about him, the miracles, the parables, the healings. When one of them would remember a detail the other had left out, they would interrupt and fill in the gaps—there was so much to remember! So much to say that they hardly even noticed when a third man joined their company. They hadn't seen him walking up behind them, but then, they had been talking so much, they wouldn't have noticed anything coming up from behind. Besides, they knew this road well, they didn't have to pay much attention.

"What are you talking about with each other as you walk?" he asked, noticing their intense conversation. And as soon as he asked, they became sad again, remembering that, as many stories as they had to tell, none of the stories could make him come back again. "Where have you been the past few days that you don't know what we're talking about?" asked Cleopas. It seemed obvious to them that everyone knew about Jesus and the way he had died. But here in front of them was one who seemed to be clueless about all of it. So they started to tell him about Jesus, about the many things he did and the way they had killed him and how now they couldn't find his body anywhere. As they finished their story, they expected this stranger to be just as sad as they were—after all, it was about the saddest story anyone could imagine.

But instead of looking sad, he started to grin. "You still don't get it, do you?" he asked them through his smile. And there on that road began the greatest of all Bible studies ever, as this stranger quoted the scriptures and explained that the Messiah, the one they were looking for and hoping for, was not one that would lead an army or shirk away from death. No, the Messiah was the One who would beat death once and for all—by dying and rising again. Life to death to life again.

That is what the scriptures said, the stranger told them matter-of-factly. They kept wanting to ask his name, but they soon forgot to even ask, as they had other questions for this wise teacher. It seemed as though they had made the journey in only minutes when they finally arrived at Emmaus, not worn out at all, but deeply stirred by the words of their new friend.

"Please stay with us," they begged him. He said he needed to be going on his way, but finally agreed to sit and eat with them. And as he sat down around the meal, he took the bread, and they both noticed how familiar his hands were. He said a blessing over the meal, and they both thought they had heard those words at least once before. He broke the bread, and a chill went through them, as they remembered a last meal with you-know-who. He handed them the bread in a way that they knew exactly who it was on the other side of the table. They suddenly knew who had been teaching them. They knew who had been walking with them. They knew who was now sharing a meal with them. And as soon as they realized it, he was gone.

He stayed with them long enough for them to figure it all out, then was on his way, leaving them to their gasping breaths and shouts of surprise. They both just stared at each other.

"That was—"

"Yeah, I know."

"Did you—"

"No."

"Me neither."

And without a word, without discussing their plans or plotting their best strategy, they both ran back out to the road, running as they had never run before, making the best time anyone had ever made on that seven-mile stretch of road. Because they had to tell their friends about the walk they had had.

Because there, in the middle of all their sorrow, in the middle of all their heartbreak, was the stranger who was no stranger at all. We could spend a lifetime guessing at the reasons they didn't know him immediately. There is something mysterious about the way God acts in our lives. Throughout scripture, people usually know when God has been somewhere, but they hardly ever know when that will happen or is actually happening.

And we are like that, too. When we give accounts of when God was active in our lives, nine out of ten times, we see God in hindsight. After the fact. We get through a tragedy, something we couldn't imagine making it through, and we realize that we were not alone. We go into surgery, scared about what will happen and uncertain about everything that is to come, and as we wake up from the anesthesia, we remember that we had a companion.

The challenge for us is the same as it was for the two walking on the road to Emmaus. Like us, they were overwhelmed with life. They knew the direction they were supposed to be taking so well that they weren't watching where they were going. Everything was routine, expected, the same.

But it was not the same road that day. Things were anything but routine, they were just the last to find out. Jesus will find each of us, too, walking along the roads of our lives, thinking that we know what is coming, thinking that we know what to expect, sure that there is nothing left that can surprise us.

This may look like the same road to you. You may think you know it by heart. But there is a difference between knowing where a road ends up and where a road is really taking you. Because when you least expect it, when you most need it, you will find yourself traveling with an unexpected companion. A friend. A teacher. A Savior. And you can bet he knows you better than you know this road.

(27) Meanwhile

After this I looked, and there was a great multitude that no one could count, from every nation, from all tribes and peoples and languages, standing before the throne and before the Lamb, robed in white, with palm branches in their hands. They cried out in a loud voice, saying, "Salvation belongs to our God who is seated on the throne, and to the Lamb!" And all the angels stood around the throne and around the elders and the four living creatures, and they fell on their faces before the throne and worshiped God, singing, "Amen! Blessing and glory and wisdom and thanksgiving and honor and power and might be to our God forever and ever! Amen." Then one of the elders addressed me, saying, "Who are these, robed in white, and where have they come from?" I said to him, "Sir, you are the one that knows." Then he said to me, "These are they who have come out of the great ordeal; they have washed their robes and made them white in the blood of the Lamb. For this reason they are before the throne of God, and worship him day and night within his temple, and the one who is seated on the throne will shelter them. They will hunger no more, and thirst no more; the sun will not strike them, nor any scorching heat; for the Lamb at the center of the throne will be their shepherd, and he will guide them to springs of the water of life, and God will wipe away every tear from their eyes." (Revelation 7:9–17)

This is the season of change, which seems like an altogether unnecessary thing to say, since, if we're honest, change is not something that comes and goes. Sometimes we are aware of the new life that is springing up around us, sometimes we can sense the dynamic transformations that are unraveling underneath our feet. Most of the time, we'd rather ignore it and pretend to be standing on our own little piece of solid ground. But whether or not we can tell or admit it's going on, we are *always* changing, always discovering the ways that things and people around us have changed. So when I say that this is the season of change, I suppose what I'm saying is that this is the season when it happens so much that we have to be honest about it—when we claim it and name it for what it is.

And change can make us do a number of odd things. We frequent the greeting card aisle in the supermarket, looking for the words we can't come up with on our own. People have babies and make job changes. They suddenly stop in the middle of what they're doing and actually think about who they are and what the hell they're doing on planet Earth. Something in the new life that surrounds us, the blooming and blossoming, stirs something deep in us. *Something silly.*

But in days like these, when change is all around us, silly is usually the best we can muster. And if you look closely, there is some real beauty hidden in the silliness. It is the time of new life and new possibility, when our senses hint at just how much potential lies below the surface. It is a time of beginnings, of commissionings.

When ships are christened for their maiden voyages, someone takes a bottle of champagne and breaks it against the hull. In many ways, it is a complete waste of time and perfectly good champagne. But I suppose if you happen to be one of those sailors who are preparing to hand their lives over to these wooden planks and the winds and the waves, trusting them to carry you out into the uncertainty of the sea and back home again, it's not so silly after all. Or maybe if you're standing there on the dock, waving goodbye to the one you love with all your heart, it makes perfect sense for all the reasons that it makes no sense at all. It's a commissioning.

Or for those of us who have one foot in the biblical story, it is something like the spilling of perfume onto a stranger's feet and wiping them with hair. A stranger who is only days away from dying a miserable death on a cross, deserted by his friends, broken, betrayed, and humiliated on top of a garbage heap. But for that moment, that sweet-smelling instant in Bethany when it seems that Jesus and that woman are the only two in the world, it is a commissioning, even if he is the only one who knows what he's being commissioned for.

And it is especially fitting that in these days of spring, when we remember all the goodbyes and endings and new beginnings that are headed our way, we dust off the Book of John's Revelation, which is, among other things, the Bible's way of saying goodbye. It is the last frame of the biblical movie, the place where heroes are supposed to ride off into the sunset and all the tension gets efficiently resolved.

Unfortunately though, Steven Spielberg didn't direct the New Testament, so when we get to these last few moments of the story, expecting a nice happy ending before the credits roll, we're in for a bit of a surprise. Because the story doesn't end.

Rather than cleaning up any loose details or answering any last-minute questions, Revelation takes whatever we thought we knew and turns it on its head. It would be enough to say some nice words about Jesus and be done with it, but instead we find ourselves standing in the midst of multi-headed dragons and bloody lambs and seven of this and seven of that. It's so confusing that rather than sending us home feeling good about what we've seen, it leaves us feeling even stranger than we did back in the Gospels. And that is why this book gets dusty. We don't really know what to do with it, so we keep it tucked away here at the end, hoping it will behave.

Of course not everyone stays away—there are many who will tell you exactly what Revelation is about—there are more books than ever claiming to know the secret formula to unwinding this awkward story. In doing a search for something else on the Internet this week, I found a new book by a pastor in my home-town that claims, among other things, that the European Union will give rise to the Antichrist and that all the barcode scanners in the supermarkets will be used to check for the mark of the Beast.

On a more mainstream level, the *Left Behind* series seems to enjoy about as much commercial success as McDonald's.

This is, of course, nothing new. Ever since Jesus left us the first time and promised to be back soon, the church in every age has thought in a sort of egocentric way that he meant right now. So every generation has come up with its own theories of how Revelation predicts that Jesus will be returning at this hour or that, as if it is some divine travel itinerary. And maybe it is, but I think to reduce this powerful story to just a math formula or a story about how we're the good guys and everyone else isn't misses the power of the thing.

The seventh chapter finds us almost in the darkest place the story has to offer. Six of the seven seals have been broken, and whatever else that means, it signals that the end is very close. The sky has grown darker and darker with each step. For those living in the world, everything around them is crumbling with death and destruction. People are turning on one another, promises are being broken, the ground itself is dying. Even the faithful few—the ones who are left that can still remember who God is or believe that God is real in such a broken and breaking world—even the faithful cry out, "How much longer, God?"

But if there is a word that sums up Revelation for me, it is this: *meanwhile.* Because for every description of the terror that engulfs the world, for every heartbreak and tragedy that happens on Earth, the story spends much more time talking about what else is going on that can't be seen. The Earth is a pit of despair and heartache, but Revelation says *meanwhile,* in the place where it matters, God is in control.

And here in the seventh chapter, those who have walked through the valley of the shadow of death, those who have stood in the midst of hell itself, and still believed, are welcomed into the company of God. They are given white robes to cover their bruises, and all the cool kisses of heaven itself for their skinned up knees. God doesn't end their crying, but is there to wipe away every tear. The world is broken, but there is a meanwhile. And so we keep this story around, even though most of the time we don't know what to do with it, because it reminds us that even the moments we think are the end are just thinly disguised beginnings. Even the moments when we feel the most helpless and hopeless, there is a meanwhile that needs to be told. It too is a commissioning.

When I went to college, I grew my hair out a bit and dressed rather stupidly, but for the most part, I was a goody-two-shoes. If you had asked me then, I would have claimed otherwise, but with the wisdom of hindsight, that's exactly what I was and exactly what I had always been. So for some reason still unknown to me, when it came time to go through fraternity rush in the first few weeks of school, I pledged the most out-of-control, animal-house fraternity that I could have. So within a few weeks of starting college, this goody-two-shoes was hanging out with characters so colorful they could only have been conceived by God. And it was the best decision I ever made—I went on being a goody-two-shoes for the most part, but those guys taught me so much about not ever taking life too seriously, about the value of friendship and the power of just being yourself because no one else could do it for you. And while I joined as many clubs and organizations as I could, running for student government and going on service trips, doing all the things I was supposed to and had always done, they just kept doing whatever it was they wanted to do that day, which didn't always involve going to class, but sometimes it did. And I was amazed. Not so much that they could break the rules, but that they could decide what they wanted for themselves, something I had long forgotten how to do.

One of the most colorful characters of those years was a friend whom I'll call Daniel. Daniel ran around the academic quad the first day of orientation hugging everyone and telling them that he loved them and they were fabulous, and I came away from that brief exchange thinking that hopefully that would be our last time together. But fate had something else in mind, and we became unlikely but very close friends.

And I could write an entire book on Daniel and the bizarre things he did that shocked the goody-two-shoes out of his own skin, like the time he found the cafeteria closed one evening so he went to knock on the door of the president's home and asked the first lady of the college to please make him a peanut butter and jelly sandwich, which to her credit, she did. Or the time he tried to make a statement about something or other (I'm not sure he

127

knew) and showed up to his English senior seminar in his boxer shorts, and only his boxer shorts. Daniel was funny and brilliant and cared not a wit for what other folks thought about him, because this is who he was, and who he had to be. And I loved him for it.

Following college, he had a number of things go wrong with family and work, and it eventually got so bad that he started trying to drink himself out of his own head. And maybe some of you know, that never really works, it only makes things worse, and so when he called me the other night in tears, he had found the bottom of his soul. He had tried to give up drinking, by cutting back to only a fifth of liquor a day, but drinking that much alone was giving him seizures. He had become violent with his wife, the first time he'd ever been violent with anyone or anything. Through slurred and sobbing words, he asked to see me. He was going to check himself into rehab, but first he needed to see me.

On the other end of the line was the father of a two-week-old baby boy. It was late. I was tired, and I didn't want to get involved. The goody-two-shoes, having remained a goody-two-shoes, has a steady job, a beautiful wife, and now a precious child. I make a mortgage payment. We have two cars that are nicer than what we need. My days have been spent worrying that we need a security system and more airbags and antibacterial soap. Maybe a moat. There is this new life in our house that I want to protect from things like alcoholism and depression. I have built up enough resistance to keep the chaos at bay, but of course, sometimes the chaos finds your phone number anyway. I agreed to meet him.

I put on some clothes and drove to a McDonald's parking lot near my house, and found Daniel there drunk, shaking with tears or withdrawal or some combination of both. I did the pastoral thing and hugged him and told him how proud I was of him, that this was the right and brave thing to do.

But you know what he said? Holding on to each other in a fast-food parking lot in the middle of the night, one drunk on alcohol, the other drunk on the idea that a mortgage payment keeps new life from breaking in, Daniel said in my ear, "I just needed to see someone who knew me better. I just had to see somebody who knew me when I wasn't like this, because I've forgotten who I am. Now I can do what I have to."

In my arms I held new life. Reeking of stale whiskey, tears streaming down his unshaved face, a career and family almost shattered—new life. Asking for a commissioning, for someone to believe there might be a meanwhile, even for him, because his capacity to believe in himself had been poisoned away.

And maybe that is what we all need, even the goody-two-shoes among us: someone to know us better. Someone to believe in us even when we can't believe in ourselves. To find smack dab in the middle of all our pain and doubt and suffering and hurt a meanwhile—another story that speaks of the promise of new life.

So here's your commissioning. It is time to go and be the people we have been called to be, trusting that even when we are hopeless, even when we are broken, even when we fail ourselves and each other, even when we think that life is done with us, there is One who knows us better.

The next time you're in worship, I hope you'll pause. It may be no more than another silly ritual, another prayer we pray because we have been told to do so, words we recite out of memory rather than passion. But my heart tells me that even as we gather, we are surrounded by a cloud of friends and witnesses, bruised but not beaten, scarred but not broken, who know what it is to be hurt and confused and to have forgotten who they are, but they also know the meanwhile—that there is a God who loves us beyond measure. And somehow knowing that story helps all the other ones make sense.

28 Last Chances

"I am the true vine, and my Father is the vinegrower. He removes every branch in me that bears no fruit. Every branch that bears fruit he prunes to make it bear more fruit. You have already been cleansed by the word that I have spoken to you. Abide in me as I abide in you. Just as the branch cannot bear fruit by itself unless it abides in the vine, neither can you unless you abide in me. I am the vine, you are the branches. Those who abide in me and I in them bear much fruit, because apart from me you can do nothing. Whoever does not abide in me is thrown away like a branch and withers; such branches are gathered, thrown into the fire, and burned. If you abide in me, and my words abide in you, ask for whatever you wish, and it will be done for you. My Father is glorified by this, that you bear much fruit and become my disciples." (John 15:1–8)

The point of reading scripture in pieces is so that you always connect yourself to the rest of the story, but you make yourself linger in that one moment, that slipping instant that holds as much truth as the whole thing put together. Even though it is still the Easter season, we read this text because we know that soon enough Jesus will again leave us, this time in a cloud, when the Ascension comes around in a few weeks. So we remember his last instructions to his friends, on the night before his death. And I think this moment at the table is one that we can understand, because it is about the surprise of goodbyes.

One of the reasons we call it the Last Supper is because it is his last chance to say anything to them, his last chance to try and explain what will happen in the next several hours, his last chance to get their attention, to offer them a word that will carry them through a hell they cannot imagine right now. And as is often the case with goodbyes, it is as much for his benefit as it is for theirs, because there is great love in him for each of them, even for the one who has just slipped out and is now running breathlessly to betray him.

Like most farewell speeches, his words ramble a bit, as he tries to clear his head of everything he wanted to say to them, only to think of one more thing and then another, never feeling as if he's said enough or the right thing. None of us are very well equipped to say the eloquent thing under such circumstances, because we are living the moment just like everyone else—we can't step back and be observers just yet. Like a careful mother desperately trying to tell the first babysitter everything she already knows. So even Jesus, in one of his more human moments, jumps all over the place, desperately reminding them to take care of unfinished business, the things that will need to be done when he is gone.

Unlike most farewells, the ones receiving the message have no idea that it's time for goodbyes. If so, they might have shown a little more reverence, taken a few more pictures, chipped in to get him a nice plant or maybe a watch. Even farther from their imagination was the idea that this goodbye would be less like a retirement party and more like a funeral, and standing before them at the edge of the cluttered table, Jesus was delivering his own eulogy. And maybe that was for the best, since none of them would be around to do it later.

Goodbyes are always hard, because they don't follow the rules. We try to prepare ourselves, to time our emotions so that we get them all out of the way and get a nice set of pictures at the same time. But often, the scheduled goodbye and the actual letting go don't coincide. You don't cry at the funeral—you feel just fine.

You're surprised at how easily you got through that, and there's a bit of pride as you comfort everyone else in their grief, feeling strong and together, but then you're folding clothes and it's there, uninvited and unexpected, and your heart stops and your stomach sinks into your socks and whereas before you had no words, no tears, suddenly they all come at once.

And I guess what I'm saying is this—for all our preparations, for all our costumes and pomp and circumstance, for all the punch and cookies and cake and cards we can throw at our goodbyes, when the real thing comes, we are always as taken off guard as the disciples were. Because while you can pencil in a hug or a last road trip on your calendar, you can't schedule the growing pains that come with change. It doesn't accept invitations.

The time that we share together, the time that we were these particular people going through these steps in our life, the moments when our roads collided and paralleled and changed because of who we became and who those around us turned out to be—those sacred moments of friendship and trust are bigger than any of our fumbling words. And those moments won't fit into a Hallmark card or a Polaroid snapshot. The only places they seem to fit are in the places we never meant to leave them, like silly old songs or ridiculous stories or random memories, and the greatest vessel of all, the human heart.

The mystery of Christ is that when we are most bruised or shaken or confused by life, when our minds and souls feel as if they can hold no more, that is when we are best able to see him, best able to hear those familiar whispers, best able to recognize that they are meant for us. So we gather around the table for a goodbye. It is not his last chance to say anything to you, but maybe we might hear him better if we acted as if it were.

"Abide in me. When you feel as if you are no one and you are going nowhere, abide in me. When you feel as if everything is right and life is bursting with possibility, abide in me. There will be times ahead when it feels as if we are far from each other, that I have forgotten you, and vice versa. But I need you to hold on, even if it feels as if your grip is shaky and you are about to tumble down even farther, hold on to me.

"I'm afraid that my presence often feels more like my absence, but such is the nature of change. Of growth. Of life and love. To be healthy is to be willing to risk everything for the sake of what is most dear. In order to heal you must be willing to hurt. To thrive is to undergo pruning. So even when it feels as if there are much better shelters than what I can offer, as if the promise is wearing thin, stick around. Abide in me. And here's the surprise—you won't be alone. For I will abide in you."

The hidden promise of the table is that while we may be surprised by the pain of goodbye, somewhere down the road we will also find each other again, different but the same, around this same table, in the surprise of hello again. Because to know Christ is to expect the unexpected, whether it's an empty tomb you're staring at or the next chapter in your life.

So goodbye, for now. Until our paths all find their way back to the promise.

29 After Pentecost: Extraordinary Time

Now what do we do?
Who are we to be?
Where have you taken us?

Our eyes adjust to the light
    two steps ahead of our souls.
Our ears strain in the silence
    our hearts afraid of what they won't find.

There. In the shadows.
The impossible takes shape
    and speaks our name.

We are not alone.

Our hearts know God best in memory, never seeing a face, only footprints and echoes. It is for our own protection, I suppose, for if our eyes were to fall on that bright presence, one wonders if they would know what to make of the sight. The stories that shape us are only tellable as we look back over our shoulders, when the lines, kept safe from change by the passage of time, can be drawn boldly. It is there, in the remembering, where God's presence is as hot as flame, as overwhelming as the cloud. The extraordinary-in-the-ordinary. The church calls it "ordinary time," one of the few moments in history where truth-in-marketing seemed to prevail.

But it is here in the rhythm and routine that God speaks most often. It is in the blank spaces on the calendar, when nothing special is happening, that the sacred breaks in. God has a special fondness for the ordinary, suggesting that there is nothing ordinary about it. So we're left with this mixed bag. Teachings, parables, stories, that don't quite fit anywhere else. It is the story that's left after we have told "the story."

It is something of a metaphor for our own experiences of God. In the end, we are never given a complete map, only scraps and clues, enough light just to see the immediate next step. Out here on the road to becoming ourselves, surrounded by this cloud of witnesses, the best we can ever muster is to take that step. To trust that the path will hold our weight and carry us into life itself. To believe in our heart of hearts that the life worth living is bigger than any one of us and that we can only truly be ourselves in the company of others. To speak our own stories into the silence, trusting that, in the end, we will look back and see a companion in the shadows.

30 The Traveler

On the way to Jerusalem Jesus was going through the region between Samaria and Galilee. As he entered a village, ten lepers approached him. Keeping their distance, they called out, saying, "Jesus, Master, have mercy on us!" When he saw them, he said to them, "Go and show yourselves to the priests." And as they went, they were made clean. Then one of them, when he saw that he was healed, turned back, praising God with a loud voice. He prostrated himself at Jesus' feet and thanked him. And he was a Samaritan. Then Jesus asked, "Were not ten made clean? But the other nine, where are they? Was none of them found to return and give praise to God except this foreigner?" Then he said to him, "Get up and go on your way; your faith has made you well." (Luke 17:11–19)

Jesus is always moving. We have to know that, not just because we are the ones who have promised him and ourselves that we would try and keep up—we have to know that because, well, it changes things. Sure, he stops every once in a while—he certainly has favorite hang-outs, places he returns to; he spends just enough time in a place to make a few friends and more than his fair share of enemies and then he is off again, moving. He began this way so long ago we often wonder if he has forgotten where he is going, if he ever knew. Of course, something in the back of our minds tells us that he knows exactly where he is going, and that only makes it more frightening. It leaves a lump in our throats to imagine that all these twisted turns might just lead somewhere. But maybe that is the thing that attracts all these people to him the most—in a life where movement seems futile if not altogether impossible, here is one who moves. Who will not or cannot stop.

And that's important for us to know, because travelers are different from the rest. Most of us would like to pretend that there's some permanence to our lives, that our families and our homes and our intelligence somehow mean unlimited stability. We are settled. Anchored. We know who we are, we know what belongs to us, we know where we belong.

People like Jesus, though—well, that's another story. How are you supposed to know who you are when you can't keep an address long enough to receive junk mail? When you are a pilgrim, you see everything differently. You belong as much in every place as you belong in any place. You *don't* belong in every place as much as you *don't* belong in any place. For most of us, it is the lines we draw around ourselves, the borders we make, that tell us who we are. It seems that we can't quite say what we are until we can say what we aren't. How are we to know where we belong, who we belong to, without knowing who we aren't? It seems as if these lines hold our very identities sometimes.

But people like Jesus, travelers, don't have much use for borders. Wanderers don't tend to care what the name of the place they're in is, they pay more attention to what other places it looks like. And when you walk everywhere you go, most places tend to look a lot alike. People may talk differently, they may eat different food, but the mark of a seasoned traveler is that they start to see similarities before they see differences.

So maybe Jesus knew where he was, maybe he didn't, maybe he did and just didn't care. I'm sure some of his followers knew exactly where they were, between Galilee and Samaria. Because that tiny stretch of land represented a much greater distance than the eye could see. The Samaritans were just close enough to the Jews in race, creed, and geography to be a real problem. And it is there, in the ambiguity of between, the great undecided, that Jesus and his followers move along, always moving, heading toward Jerusalem.

While it was nowhere to most of the people that made their way through, it was home to at least a few. The ten had become friends, I suppose, in the way that people in crisis band together. It was necessity really—their families had abandoned them, their faith communities had abandoned them, they were a people without a place to belong. So it was appropriate that they made their home in no place, here in the middle of two very different regions, suffering through their leprosy and surviving off the mercy of travelers. They had seen all kinds come through there—it was quite the first-century highway these days—some people looked down and walked faster, some stopped and stared—children particularly were amazed at how disfigured these strangers were. But every once in a while, someone would come along who felt like being generous and would toss them a scrap of food or some money or anything else they didn't especially need for themselves.

They had managed to establish quite a routine, these ten—not a one of them could remember how it all began, but they had begun to accept that this was their fate, as dark and empty as it seemed, to live not on either side of the border, but in the border itself. Claimed by no one, wanted by no one, the in-betweens.

And so that Monday evening or Thursday morning or Saturday night, whenever it was, that the traveler came along, it should have been business as usual. They'd keep their distance, shout out their requests, hope for the best. But this traveler was different, and somehow they knew that. Not everyone knew it—in fact, most people never noticed him as he walked around—but those living in pain, whether emotional, physical, spiritual—they could see him. Somehow without a word, without credentials, without seeing him do anything else other than walk toward them, they had reason to shout. *Jesus, Master, have mercy on us!*

Maybe it even surprised them when it came out of their own mouths, or maybe they weren't sure what they expected his mercy to be, but they knew it was something they had to have. *Jesus, Master, have mercy on us!*

I imagine they were more than just a little disappointed when his only response was, "Go to the temple. Let the priests see you." They detected in his tone an almost aloofness, as if his mind was already somewhere else, as if his heart was two steps ahead of his

139

feet. *Go to the temple? What, so we can be told again how unclean we are? So we can be rejected all over again? Maybe we were wrong about this one.* But something in them, the same thing that let them see this traveler for what he was, set them to walking.

They were all quiet at first, wondering about what the fellow had said, why he had wanted this, wondering what the others were thinking. They thought of their families, the last time they had seen the inside of the temple. And as their minds wandered, as their steps fell into rhythm, something changed. It would not be right for me to try to describe it in my own words. I doubt that if they were here they could even do it justice—something just changed. That's what you need to know. That on that road between nowhere to somewhere, these ten found healing.

But one of them—one found more than just the end of his pain. There is healing, and then there is *healing*. And for whatever reason, this one out of ten, this Samaritan, this nobody without a name or a home, could not keep walking with the rest. Maybe his suffering had been greater, maybe he knew something the others didn't, maybe he just knew that his religious expression wouldn't be welcome at the temple. Or maybe he knew this was his only chance to thank the traveler. The one who had crossed boundaries and ignored borders and healed the unhealable. The one who also knew no home. The one who also had no people. The one who also lived between borders.

And that one, the strange wandering nomad walking in circles to reach his destination, making his way to the crossroads of life and death itself, can only laugh at the irony of it all. "I remember ten. Weren't there ten? I count one, now. And this one—why this one is Samaritan! How about that. Get up, friend, it's time to go home. Get on your way then."

For those of us caught in between, unsure of who we are, where we are going: get ready. For those of us who have lost hope in change, lost hope in everything that once meant something to us, lost hope in ourselves: get ready. Because when we least expect it, the traveler will come this way. And the irony of it is that we who are brokenhearted, we who do not know how to make sense of our own lives, much less the mysteries of heaven and earth, we will be the ones with eyes to see and ears to hear. Get ready.

31 What the Bread Says

John said to him, "Teacher, we saw someone casting out demons in your name, and we tried to stop him, because he was not following us." But Jesus said, "Do not stop him; for no one who does a deed of power in my name will be able soon afterward to speak evil of me. Whoever is not against us is for us. For truly I tell you, whoever gives you a cup of water to drink because you bear the name of Christ will by no means lose the reward. If any of you put a stumbling block before one of these little ones who believe in me, it would be better for you if a great millstone were hung around your neck and you were thrown into the sea. If your hand causes you to stumble, cut it off; it is better for you to enter life maimed than to have two hands and to go to hell, to the unquenchable fire. And if your foot causes you to stumble, cut it off; it is better for you to enter life lame than to have two feet and to be thrown into hell. And if your eye causes you to stumble, tear it out; it is better for you to enter the kingdom of God with one eye than to have two eyes and to be thrown into hell, where their worm never dies, and the fire is never quenched. For everyone will be salted with fire. Salt is good; but if salt has lost its saltiness, how can you season it? Have salt in yourselves, and be at peace with one another." (Mark 9:38–50)

Bread is not especially exciting.

I cannot, off the top of my head, come up with any movies that have been made about bread; I have never personally been to a bread convention, belonged to any kind of bread fan club. As far as I know bread was not used in any of the Olympic sports. You get my point. It's just bread. There's not that much you can say about it. A rather plain and unexciting mixture of plain and unexciting ingredients.

And so it's a bit strange that the Bible spends so much time talking about bread:

- In the Exodus of the Israelites from Egypt, manna, perhaps the most unexciting member of the bread family, falls from the sky daily, keeping the people fed and mindful of their dependence on the invisible provider.

- When Jesus teaches his disciples how to pray, the one thing he tells them to ask for—not health or world peace or more faith—is their daily share of bread.

- In his struggle to help the disciples and others understand who he is and what he is about, he calls himself the "bread of life."

- And of course, when he sits down to tell his disciples goodbye at their last meal together, he breaks bread. He has been trying to help them understand what will happen for days and weeks and months, but somehow it is only in the sharing of the bread that they begin to "get it." The act of sharing bread seems to say it better than even Jesus' own words can.

We spend a lot of time talking about how in the communion meal the ordinary becomes extraordinary. Plain old bread from the Piggly Wiggly store, made by hands unaware of their own significance, somehow mysteriously reminds us of the amazing. The very plain becomes incredible.

But what is even more amazing to me these days is how the extraordinary becomes plain. That somehow all the mystery and expansive love of God can be wholly contained in a piece of bread and some cheap wine. Everything you need to hear is somewhere in there—you are loved, God cares for you, God will provide, etcetera, etcetera—along with a slew of question marks and unfinished sentences to keep you hungry for more.

Because the great thing about bread is that you never can get enough. It's not like climbing Mt. Everest, graduating from college, or winning a gold medal. While all those things may tout themselves to be amazing accomplishments, bread makes no such promises. You cannot get your fill in one sitting. You have to come back to this table again and again and again, getting just enough to carry you to the next time. This bread is a promise that there is peace for the hunger within you.

And while that may sound like a simple message, it can be one of the hardest to hear. It seems that most of the time we want God's love to be complex, intricate, so that some of us (read: *me*) who spent a bunch of time and money on a seminary education have a leg up on everybody else.

And this is not new. The Gospel lesson reminds us of that. At this point in the story, the disciples, who are usually pretty confused, have now come to a place called "completely clueless." The disciples and Jesus are operating on completely separate levels. While Jesus continues to describe his fatal future, the disciples bicker over who is the employee of the month. While Jesus uses a child to show that the weak will be given a special place in his kingdom, the disciples argue over who the best disciple is. They want to be assured that their closeness to Jesus, their in-crowd status, gives them some privileges in his eyes. So when they see someone else, a non-disciple, using Jesus' name to heal people, they flip out, because this woman or man is not a card-carrying member. Not one of us. Different. They should be sued for disciple malpractice.

But Jesus' reaction is not to seek out the outsider, or even to act surprised. Instead, Jesus lets out some powerfully simple words: Whoever is not against us is for us. Jesus' calm acceptance of the stranger reminds the disciples that the power to heal comes from the name of Jesus, not Peter or James or John or Brian. It is the name of the master, not the name of the servant that is important. Membership is not determined by special privilege or unique gifts—just action in the name of Christ. Even giving a cup of water in the name of Jesus will not go unnoticed. It is simple, but powerful. The disciples are suddenly not alone.

Whenever we gather around the bread and the cup, we are reminded that we are not the only ones who gather around this table. We are not the only ones hungry. We are not the only ones who look upon simple loaves of bread and see hope for the world. Though we cannot see them, we are surrounded by the faces and hearts of countless millions.

Some of them look just like you or me, some of them are different colors, some have names I would never try to pronounce. Some live in houses of brick and wood, some under mud and thatch, some have no place to call home. Some will eat official churchy-looking bread that cracks loudly when you break it, some will eat rice or corn or whatever they can find, some will not have bread to break. But we all gather around one table, in the hopes that the One who called us here will feed us.

While our world aches with the sounds of police sirens, guns, the rumbling of empty stomachs, and the breaking of hearts, we gather to remember that there is more going on than what is immediately visible. There is real hope. Peace is possible. Life wins. God still loves the world. And while our words cannot say everything we would hope to, we trust that this simple and plain and unexciting loaf of bread says it all.

32 Jesus Is Lord

So Moses cried out to the LORD, "What shall I do with this people? They are almost ready to stone me." The LORD said to Moses, "Go on ahead of the people, and take some of the elders of Israel with you; take in your hand the staff with which you struck the Nile, and go. I will be standing there in front of you on the rock at Horeb. Strike the rock, and water will come out of it, so that the people may drink." Moses did so, in the sight of the elders of Israel. He called the place Massah and Meribah, because the Israelites quarreled and tested the LORD, saying, "Is the LORD among us or not?" (Exodus 17:4–7)

If then there is any encouragement in Christ, any consolation from love, any sharing in the Spirit, any compassion and sympathy, make my joy complete: be of the same mind, having the same love, being in full accord and of one mind. Do nothing from selfish ambition or conceit, but in humility regard others as better than yourselves. Let each of you look not to your own interests, but to the interests of others. Let the same mind be in you that was in Christ Jesus, who, though he was in the form of God, did not regard equality with God as something to be exploited, but emptied himself, taking the form of a slave, being born in human likeness. And being found in human form, he humbled himself and became obedient to the point of death—even death on a cross. Therefore God also highly exalted him and gave him the name that is above every name, so that at the name of Jesus every knee should bend, in heaven and on earth and under the earth, and every tongue should confess that Jesus Christ is Lord, to the glory of God the Father. Therefore, my beloved, just as you have always obeyed me, not only in my presence, but much more now in my absence, work out your own salvation with fear and trembling; for it is God who is at work in you, enabling you both to will and to work for his good pleasure. (Philippians 2:1–13)

For some reason, I've been thinking a lot lately about the way I preach. This particularly hits me hard when it's time to speak on scriptures like this Philippians passage, because I hear in my head all the three-point sermons that have ever been delivered. I remember my great-grandmother summarizing her thoughts on preachers and preaching by saying that, "as long as they say Jesus is Lord a few times, I feel like I've been to church." I very rarely say stuff like "Jesus is Lord." It's not that I don't believe it, it's that I think it's a trap. It seems so easy to say. We hear it all the time in churches and from pulpits, we print it on bumper stickers, we sing it in songs, we have it engraved on coffee mugs. It seems as easy as saying "It's everywhere you want to be" or "We love to fly and it shows."

But if you're like me, the product of an educational system that taught you a lot of great things, but the thing that sticks out the most is *be critical of everything you see and take it apart in your head until you develop a clinical migraine*, nothing is as easy as it seems. To say that Jesus is Lord is not just to say that you think Jesus is a nice guy who said some good things. It's not just to say that you think Jesus died and was brought back to more than life. It certainly includes those things, but to say that Jesus is Lord is to say something much more profound and mysterious and frightening than all our bumper stickers could.

To say that Jesus is Lord is to declare that the world doesn't work the way we think it does. That something is broken with reality, and the only way to fix it is to break it some more. It is saying that the way to light is through darkness, the way to truth is through confusion, the way to life is through death. And the

146

trickiest thing about it is that as soon as you figure out what it means, it means something else. It's like one of those pull-string dolls that randomly spits out some saying, but you never know what you're getting when you pull the cord. It's like learning Spanish so you can talk to your next-door neighbor, only to find out he speaks Portuguese. It is not the kind of truth you find in the mitosis section of your biology textbook, not the kind of truth you can memorize and store away in your pocket. You can no more keep it to yourself than you can hold love, or taste sunlight, or decide where the wind will blow.

And rightly so, that freaks some people out. Frankly, I worry more about the people who don't get freaked out by it. The ones who don't have a problem wearing Christian T-shirts that were made by children in Honduras. The ones who see no disconnect between their faith in a Messiah crucified by the authorities and the idea that their country is more important than every other people or place. But in the end, we are like the Pharisees who want to trap Jesus in a war of words. We want answers. People want a faith they can put their hands on. They want to trust in something they can see.

The Israelites were like that. And so God led them on in the form of a cloud, then a pillar of fire. But when the excitement wore off, in a matter of weeks, they were more interested in food than the presence of God. And by the time they come to Massah and Meribah, they are convinced God is not with them. They cry out, "Is the Lord among us or not?" These who have seen the Red Sea part, manna and quail fall from the sky, and now water pour out of a rock like a fire hydrant, are asking "Is the Lord among us or not?" Later, their children and their children's children's children would tell these stories again, because they saw what their ancestors couldn't—the clear presence of a living God. And that is the funny thing about God. In a few weeks, Moses will ask to see God, and God's answer is for Moses to hide in the face of a rock, and God will pass by. The lesson is that the most you will ever see of God is in hindsight. Don't expect to see God coming. Don't plan on knowing every time God is around. Usually our best tools in the search for God are artifacts and fingerprints, stories and memory. But in the end, even these are only tools. When we find God, it will be through no effort of our own, but maybe our searching will have given us eyes to recognize when God passes our way.

So when we say "Jesus is Lord," we're not so much saying that we know what Jesus is up to, or we have plans for what Jesus will do tomorrow. Christ will not be our puppet. In fact, to say that Christ is Lord is to say that none of the rules apply, that our wisdom is more of a best guess than a sure bet. That the cross is more of a question mark than an exclamation point. It is to say that despite our deep need for security and stability and possessions and definition, we've decided to stay on this road at least a few more miles. Walking two steps behind, searching the ground for footprints, adjusting and readjusting our eyes to the clouded darkness. Knowing somewhere deep inside us, in the place we can't always describe or understand, that Jesus is Lord. May our hearts and actions and lives tell it to the world.

33 Telling the Good Guys from the Bad Guys

He also told this parable to some who trusted in themselves that they were righteous and regarded others with contempt: "Two men went up to the temple to pray, one a Pharisee and the other a tax collector. The Pharisee, standing by himself, was praying thus, 'God, I thank you that I am not like other people: thieves, rogues, adulterers, or even like this tax collector. I fast twice a week; I give a tenth of all my income.' But the tax collector, standing far off, would not even look up to heaven, but was beating his breast and saying, 'God, be merciful to me, a sinner!' I tell you, this man went down to his home justified rather than the other; for all who exalt themselves will be humbled, but all who humble themselves will be exalted." (Luke 18:9–14)

There are words in our Christian vocabulary that fit us like old shoes. They fit us as much as we fit them. We know what to expect from them—they are reliable, we can say them and everyone around us will know what we are talking about. Words that are comfortable and familiar—words that we trust. I am particularly thinking of the word *prayer*.

Prayer is part of the "old standby" vernacular of the Christian tradition, and we frequently have no problem throwing it around as if everyone knows exactly what we're talking about. We are especially apt to do that in worship. We say, "Let us pray," and we don't pause for a question and answer period. We don't hand out instruction cards. It would probably feel awkward if we did—like the one-millionth time you hear the flight attendant verbally unravel the immensely complicated mystery known as the seatbelt. Surely people know how to do this, right? We all learned prayers as kids, *Now I lay me down to sleep* and all that—we all chant together the one prayer he left for us without much trouble.

As someone who is called on to pray every once in a while, I can assure you that you can pray for just about anything. I have prayed for luncheons, business meetings, even basketball games. Looking through the prayer books of any given denomination will quickly teach you that there are prayers for any possible occasion. It's not as if you need a prayer license or any sort of special training. We frequently hold silence in worship, trusting each one to find their own prayer, do their own thing. *Everybody* understands what prayer is.

So we are smart enough to know better than the Pharisee. We know not to tell God we are better than everyone else. We know that every once in a while we ought to remember how much we've screwed up—that's what the "prayer of confession" is for. This story is so obvious from the very beginning—who's the good guy and who's the bad guy—it's even less complicated than the airplane seatbelt. We get it. Can we go home?

Of course—as always—there is a catch. His name is Jesus, and he frequents these places we like to settle down into. It's like sitting down in your favorite chair only to have him point out that it's actually on fire. He takes the most beautiful landscapes we know and fills them with landmines—things we didn't expect and most of the time didn't want to see at all. He is especially bad about doing this in the Gospel of Luke, where the good news seems to be wrapped up in reversal. Everything changes. Nothing is as it seems.

But here, 2,000 years on the other side of that good news, surely we've reversed all we needed to. We know that the Pharisees are really the crooks and the tax collectors are just misunderstood but basically okay guys. We know all the trite little phrases about the last being first and the boss being a servant and blessed are the poor. We know how it works. We know the story before it starts, but to be polite, we will humor Jesus and listen one more time.

The temple is crowded as usual, so crowded that we are barely able to think, much less move. It is not a quiet place, not a particularly contemplative place, at least not as far as we are concerned. It is hot and smelly and confusing. It feels more like a circus than a place of worship. And here, scattered about, you can find all different kinds of people who have come from all different kinds of places for all different kinds of reasons. Some have come to buy or sell things, some have come to sell themselves. Many, and maybe most, have come to pray. And like us, they pretty much know what that means. At least one of them does, and as he walks by in his simple robe and focused expression, we would never guess that it's . . . *the Pharisee.*

We expected him to look more like a "bad guy." An eye patch or a curly mustache or something. Some clear marker that indicates he's no good. But there is no such indicator. Here is just a simple man who has given his life over to God and his faith. Completely. And as he walks into the temple, he is so grateful for the choices he has made. He doesn't do it intentionally, but it's hard not to notice all the squalor around—the temple gets worse everyday, it seems, and he is just so thankful that he is not a part of it. That he lives in a safe neighborhood. That he knows God. That he knows how to pray. Looking over the chaos that surrounds him, he is keenly aware of his blessings. And as he makes his way to the center of the temple, where he can get some space to himself and think clearly, he brushes up against some of the chaos.

Namely, an old tax collector. And while it is tempting to paint him as a sympathetic character, I'm not sure Jesus meant for us to. He is just a tax collector. He is powerful. He preys on the weak. He has sold out his own people to make money. In many ways, he is no different from Judas Iscariot—an enterprising fellow who has never been very popular and doesn't really care to be. Who knows why he's here? Maybe he's in town for a conference and just wandered in, or maybe he's one of these that just lost someone really important and has come for a temporary fix of faith—after all, that is when we are all best at praying, when the reality of life doesn't quite match the glossy brochure. No one forced this man to be a tax collector, and so it's hard to have much pity on him now that he's upset. And maybe no one knows that better than the tax collector himself, who can only cry out: "God if you are there, give me a break. I don't deserve it. I know that much. Just please—have mercy."

He does not know the proper forms. He hasn't been in here long enough to know any of the psalms. He just says what he feels, much like those people who are so upset they have nothing else to say other than Jesus' name. And we get upset because we feel it has somehow offended our careful sensibilities, but there is something very real underneath that crude surface. A crying out. A deep need. A hunger for something more real.

The tax collector is not a good guy. The Pharisee is not a bad guy. It would not be gospel if that were so. The thing that makes this good news is that it is surprising news. There is a revolution afoot, says Jesus. Those who have every reason to trust in themselves will learn that none of those things matter very much in the long run. Those who seem to have nothing, and realize it, will have the greatest gift of all—dependence. Dependence on the God who hears prayer, however crude, however misguided, however theologically unsophisticated. So if you are confused about prayer, if you don't know what you're doing most of the time, if you have time for everything except that which is most important, find some peace in this: It is not about who you are. It is not about what you do. It would be so much simpler if it were. It seems that it is more about *why* you are.

Unless you happen to be the Dalai Lama, none of us are able to carry that clarity around with us all of the time—but we are each given moments of deep humility, when we know we are standing only by that invisible and unspoken grace. We can't always name it. We can't usually say anything intelligent about it. But we can feel it. And in those moments, when we are less and that unnamed miracle is more, we would be wise then to stop and count our blessings.

34 God Will Take Care of It

Isaac said to his father Abraham, "Father!" And he said, "Here I am, my son." He said, "The fire and the wood are here, but where is the lamb for a burnt offering?" Abraham said, "God himself will provide the lamb for a burnt offering, my son." So the two of them walked on together. When they came to the place that God had shown him, Abraham built an altar there and laid the wood in order. He bound his son Isaac, and laid him on the altar, on top of the wood. Then Abraham reached out his hand and took the knife to kill his son. But the angel of the LORD called to him from heaven, and said, "Abraham, Abraham!" And he said, "Here I am." He said, "Do not lay your hand on the boy or do anything to him; for now I know that you fear God, since you have not withheld your son, your only son, from me." (Genesis 22:7–12)

If the story ended with Abraham and Sarah taking baby Isaac home from the hospital, it would be an easier story to tell. If they had just walked off into the sunset with a happy ending, it would be an easier story to tell.

There are some moments in the Bible that are so dark, where God seems so hidden, that we would rather avoid them altogether. We'd prefer just to hang out in the scriptures that make us feel alright about ourselves, like 1 Corinthians 13—who can argue with that? Or when Jesus invites the little children to come closer to him. That's a nice moment. Nobody gets hurt, there are no tears, no unanswered questions. Those kinds of warm and cozy moments are what we love about the Bible. But occasionally, we step in there looking for happy and fuzzy, and all we find is cold and prickly.

Because the Bible is about all of life, not just the moments when everything makes sense. Not just the moments when we feel good about things or things are going our way. It is meant to teach us that God is in all our moments, our moments of great joy and our deepest bouts of despair. Fear. Self-doubt. Anger. Because it is only in spending time in the Bible's dark places that our eyes will learn to see through the shadows. To see through the darkness the faint outline of a God who waits with us through all our sorrow.

Abraham makes the angel repeat himself three times, not believing what he hears. But every time, it comes out the same: "Take your child, Isaac, your only son, your pride and joy, to Moriah. Don't tell Sarah what you're doing. And when you get there, take his life."

For what seems like hours after the angel leaves, Abraham buries his face in his hands and sobs. He cries out in anger, pleading with God, but there is no answer. Just silence. So, a few hours before daybreak, he climbs the stairs like someone in a trance, and opens the door to Isaac's room. He stares at him in the darkness, then gently strokes his head to wake him up. Unable to look his son in the eye, he tells him to get dressed, that they're going to Moriah for a surprise hunting trip, and to be quiet so that they don't wake his mother.

Once they're in Abraham's pickup, they head toward the woods, Isaac sitting next to his father on the bench seat. He is excited, like any boy would be, to spend the day with his father, but every time he asks Abraham a question, Abraham just stares blankly at the road ahead and mumbles back, "God will take care of it. God will take care of it."

They pull into the gravel parking lot a few hours later, just at the head of the trail. Isaac jumps out of the truck, thrilled and impatient, telling his dad to hurry up. But Abraham just sits in the driver's seat, his hand still resting on the steering wheel, his eyes still staring straight ahead. As if he's moving through quicksand, he unlatches his seatbelt, opens the door, and steps out of the cab. In his hand is his rifle case, as he and Isaac start to make their way down the trail, just as the sun is starting to shine through the tall trees.

Isaac is young enough to notice everything as if it is brand new. Every bird. Every leaf on every tree. He explains to his dad what his teacher taught him about how the plants get their energy from the sun's rays, but Abraham hears none of it, as he mumbles to himself, "God will take care of it."

When they finally make it to the first clearing, Abraham whispers to his son in a cracking voice to run on ahead, that he'll catch up to him in a minute. As soon as his son sprints off into the field, Abraham's tears return in full force. He remembers holding him for the first time in the delivery room. The cake Sarah made for his first birthday party. The images race through his mind like a spinning film reel. There are so many memories, so many tears, that he can barely see what he is doing.

I can't tell you where the strength comes from to take his rifle from the case and load a single shot. I'm not sure Abraham could even tell you. I can't tell you whether it's faith or insanity that allows him to lift the scope to his teary eye and rest his trembling finger on the trigger. The story doesn't tell us any of that. It doesn't tell us what Abraham was thinking or feeling as he aimed at his target. All it tells us is his prayer, the same prayer he'd been mumbling ever since he first saw the angel: "God will take care of it."

And there, in that darkest of moments, when Abraham looks upon the blessing he's been given and is ready to destroy it, to take his own son's life, two things happen.

The first is that, for whatever reason, Isaac turns around and sees his father aiming the gun at him. He doesn't run. He doesn't even move. He just stares back, his brown eyes looking just like Abraham's in their trance. He looks at his dad with a mixture of hurt, fear, and confusion. And their eyes meet.

The second thing that happens is that God breaks the silence. Abraham hears the sweetest words he has ever heard. *Put the gun down.* It is the voice of God, telling Abraham that he has proven himself, proven his love in the most powerful way possible: he was willing to take a life even more precious to him than his own. A few thousand years later, God would understand Abraham's feeling of helplessness all too well, watching his own son cry out, "Why have you abandoned me?"

Abraham drops the rifle and falls to his knees. After a few minutes, Isaac slowly approaches him, not sure whether he should run from him or embrace him, but before he can decide, Abraham grabs him and holds onto him as if his life depended on it. Pulling him to his chest, Abraham cries out his prayer one last time: "God will take care of it." Before they leave that day, for a very quiet and awkward ride home, Abraham takes a rock and carves into the side of the mountain the words "El-Yireh"—God will take care of it.

I have to tell you that as I was writing this, there was a certain three-month-old cooing next to me on the bed, grabbing the corners of my pages and wrapping his tiny fingers around them. Before he was born, I didn't understand this story. Now I can say with confidence that I absolutely don't understand this story.

If this were to happen today, we would all cheer when Abraham was locked up and put away for child abuse. We would plaster his wrinkled face across every tabloid front page. One more crazy person hearing voices and doing horrible things to children.

But it's not in the newspaper, it's in the Bible. And it's not just Abraham's behavior that's disturbing to me—*it's God's*. It's the way God tests Abraham in the cruelest way possible. If God knows us all so well, didn't he already know that Abraham would go through with it? Didn't he already know how deep Abraham's faith went? Why put him and all of us through such a horrible moment?

For what it's worth, here is my best guess, as a full-time father and a part-time Christian. This is not a story of God testing Abraham, as much as it is a story of Abraham testing God. While God might have known how deep Abraham's faith went, Abraham did not. He didn't know how deep it went until he looked into the face of the thing he loved most in all the world, the life he loved more than his own, in the darkest and most frightening moment of his life, and found that God was there with him. That God would take care of it.

That's how Abraham learned it. I learned that lesson from my grandmother.

When I was growing up, there was no better sight in the world than the highway streetlights at the entrance to Selma, Alabama, because it meant that we'd made it to Grannie and Daddy Charles's house. I grew up convinced that they were the wealthiest relatives I had, not just because they spoiled me rotten, but because their house seemed to lack for nothing. Later on, when I was older, I would discover that by most standards they had very little, but their house was full of an incredible love.

It was their love for each other, the way they cared for one another, that helped me to know when I had found the woman I wanted to spend the rest of my life with. Nothing was more important in that house than family and faith. My grandmother, before she retired, was a secretary at their conservative little Southern Baptist congregation for almost a half-century. They were there together every time the doors were open, and most of the time they were the ones opening the doors.

Every time I visited my grandparents, I took my place in the children's Sunday school class, intimidated by the kids who were much better at their "scripture drills" and verse memorization. It felt more like a gun safety class than it did a holy communion with the Almighty, as if they were preparing for an impending military drill with Jesus. It was my first introduction to the theological complexities that separate the Body of Christ. It was clear they were talking about the same God I had grown up with, but doing so in a manner that didn't jibe with the God I knew. But I loved my grandparents, and they loved that church. I would put up with a little discomfort if it meant being in their company.

But when my grandfather was diagnosed with a terminal brain tumor, both family and faith took a blow. For two years, we all watched that strong and proud man slowly wither away in front of our eyes. The doctors kept saying it would be any time now, but he kept on going. Even when everything around it was shutting down, his heart kept on beating. My grandmother said it's because it just didn't know any better.

Twenty years ago this November, he finally passed away, just 56 years old. There are certainly more tragic losses in the history of humanity, but you would be hard pressed to convince my family.

I was only nine when he died, but from the day he passed, my grandmother loved all of us for the two of them. She kept him alive in her stories, trying to give us the encouragement and advice he might have given us if he had seen us grow up. She shared his stories, so that it was almost as if he were there. But she also suffered a great deal. It is difficult to breathe for two people, and that's almost what she did for us. My grandfather was more than a husband to her, he was her best friend, her deepest joy.

Last Easter, my wife and I went to stay with her for the weekend down in Selma, and on Saturday morning, I got up early and found her already awake, watching television. We started out talking about nothing in particular, but eventually our conversation turned to faith. She told me that when Charles died, so many people told her it was for the best, that God had wanted it this way, that she almost couldn't go to church anymore. It was suffocating, all the people who were telling her exactly where God was in her pain. She was so very sad, but she was also angry, and she didn't know whom to be angry with.

Until one morning in Sunday school, when the pastor of that little Southern Baptist church asked her class if anyone had ever been angry with God. Figuring it must be some sort of trick question, no one said anything at first, but then one lone hand went up in the air. It was my grandmother's. And as we sat there in her living room, she told me that it was only then that she realized that God was big enough to hold all of her pain and doubt and anger, along with all her joy and happiness—only then did she understand that God's arms were big enough for all her broken pieces, and only then did her heart begin to heal.

Doctors will tell you that every time you feel pain in your body, it is because something has gotten disconnected that wasn't supposed to be. All pain comes from separation, and the most profound pain in our lives comes when we feel distance from God.

When Christ breaks the bread, when Christ breaks his own body, it is a way of saying that even in the brokenness, even in the deepest darknesses of our lives, God will be there. No matter what is weighing on you. No matter how much loss you've suffered, no matter what mistakes you've made, there is hope for healing. There is hope for resurrection. For God taking all these broken pieces of our lives, and mending them back together. God will take care of it. God will take care of it.

We lost my grandmother this past summer. She had a cancer that the doctors didn't detect until it was much too late, so within a week of her diagnosis, she slipped into a coma and died. It had spread so rapidly that they told us she really shouldn't have made it that long, but we knew what they didn't, that she shared a heart with her husband Charles, and like his, hers just didn't know any better.

Near her bed in the hospital when she died was a picture of her holding her new great-grandson Henry, who shares a middle name with her husband. Henry won't remember that picture being taken, but I'm going to make sure that he knows her all the same, that I keep her alive for him in my stories, so that her heart might beat in his tiny chest, too. So that when the time comes for him to pass through the broken and dark places, he will find the courage to see that figure in the shadows. The God who stands with us in all our pain. The God who can hold together all our fragile pieces, no matter how desperate we feel. The God who makes sense of the senseless.

God will take care of it. God will take care of it.

35   On Being Found

Now all the tax collectors and sinners were coming near to listen to him. And the Pharisees and the scribes were grumbling and saying, "This fellow welcomes sinners and eats with them." So he told them this parable: "Which one of you, having a hundred sheep and losing one of them, does not leave the ninety-nine in the wilderness and go after the one that is lost until he finds it? When he has found it, he lays it on his shoulders and rejoices. And when he comes home, he calls together his friends and neighbors, saying to them, 'Rejoice with me, for I have found my sheep that was lost.' Just so, I tell you, there will be more joy in heaven over one sinner who repents than over ninety-nine righteous persons who need no repentance. Or what woman having ten silver coins, if she loses one of them, does not light a lamp, sweep the house, and search carefully until she finds it? When she has found it, she calls together her friends and neighbors, saying, 'Rejoice with me, for I have found the coin that I had lost.' Just so, I tell you, there is joy in the presence of the angels of God over one sinner who repents."
(Luke 15:1–10)

The funny thing about being lost is that you're usually not ready to admit to yourself that is what you are. Something in my chromosome makeup demands that I drive at least a full hour out of my way before stopping and asking for directions. What my wife (and other frighteningly reasonable people in my life) cannot seem to understand is that to do so, to stop and ask where it was that I drove off the map, would be to admit defeat, and that is simply unacceptable.

At some point in my development, the idea got planted into my head that since the world is round, all roads must eventually lead back to one another. Given that bulletproof logic, it makes perfect sense that if you keep going down the wrong road, you will eventually end up on the right one. This is the school of thought that says you can never really be lost, as long as you remain confident that you know where you're going. In this way of thinking, being lost is not so much a state of being as it is a state of mind. Yet after almost three decades of driving down the wrong roads, they have yet to lead back to the right one.

And this doesn't just apply to driving. Being lost is not just about being in an unknown physical location—it's no accident that Jesus used the concept to describe those who needed God the most. Most of the time, we just have no idea where our spiritual lives are taking us. We work so hard to understand God, to search for God, to make ourselves more devoted to God. We make our faith about something we do, some person we are. I have had plenty of friends along the way who changed their lives completely trying to grow closer to God. In the few years I have worked with college students as a chaplain, I have counseled innumerable students who gave up all their friends because they weren't Christian enough. There is this intense pressure in some Christian circles that if you're going to be Christian, you've got to change your environment altogether, otherwise how will your faith survive?

The church has a word for this, works righteousness. It treats the love of God like some fragile piece of china that might break at any moment. Therefore everything in your life has to have the edges taken off, so that your faith can survive. It means that you think the love of God can be earned, that if you try hard enough, you will find God on your own, whether it's through Bible study or prayer or community service or worship or whatever. And while all of that certainly helps you grow closer to God, it's more complex than that.

Because God is sort of unpredictable. If you want to observe a wild animal in its natural habitat, you do not drive into the woods in your SUV, subwoofers blazing, lay on the horn and demand that the animal show itself. That usually won't even work in a zoo, much less the forest. It's sort of the same thing with God. Everything we do to facilitate an experience of God is important, but in the end, it's up to God. Sometimes faith is not doing anything, but allowing something to happen. It's not finding our own way back onto the map, it's slowing down long enough to drink deeply of our lost-ness.

Because finally, you must admit—you're lost. Maybe it's been a while now, maybe it just happened. A few signs way back looked familiar, but even retracing your steps would be futile at this point. It's getting dark, there is a cold breeze, unfamiliar sounds surround you. Your heart longs for a familiar voice, a familiar face, your stomach growls for the smells and tastes of home. So maybe you wander into a church. Maybe there's something there that can get you back on the path you were looking for, but as you spend more time there, you discover that most of those people are just as lost as you are, but many of them won't even admit it. So you head out on your own again, gritting your teeth against the cold and uncertainty of this roundabout journey you seem stuck on.

And most days, when you get your rhythm down, when your pace isn't upset by bumps in the road or sudden storms, you can pretend very well that you know where it is you're going. But when pain comes, when loneliness sets in, you know all too well how little you really know.

When the lectionary brought us around to this story in September 2001, it happened to be just five days after one of the darkest days in American history. That happened to be a rather unusual week, as you may remember. Churches packed their pews with folks looking for answers, trying to make sense of the horrible plane crashes and crumbling buildings that kept flashing on their television screens. Some of us sitting in those pews were still shocked. We had no emotional or mental resources to make sense of what had happened. Others had seen enough to just be angry, and they were ready for vengeance against an unseen enemy.

Regardless of what we were feeling that week, we took our places and opened the Bible to this story that used to just be a simple parable, but we found in the days that had transpired, we had new ears for its message. Because where before we had seen shepherds and sheep, a woman and her coin, we now saw firefighters and rubble, dust-covered volunteers frantically searching for just one survivor, hoping that if they could just find one, maybe it would light a candle in the face of such great darkness. "Lost" took on a whole new meaning for all of us, as did the hope of finding and being found.

We think of those lost beneath the dust and debris, we think of those around the world so lost in their own hate that they would support such unspeakable terror or so lost in their own vengefulness that they would ask our government to carry out equally horrific violence, indifferent to justice. When suffering and hatred and violence and sadness and destruction and all the other emotions we drank so deeply in those days, when they come our way, we know for certain what we have guessed for a long time is true—none of us know where we're going. We woke up on a normal Tuesday morning to a world that was not the same.

And in many ways, we've moved on. Our hearts are a little tougher, we are a little more accustomed to seeing terrorism on TV, a little more callous to the cries of war. Even our memories of that dark Tuesday don't slow us down as much anymore. We've seen those awful images of fire and rubble enough to be ready for them. While the tragedy closed everything down that week in 2001, the anniversaries that have followed have been little more than blips on the cultural radar for most. Businesses remain open, there are sporadic prayers and memorial services, but for the most part, it is life as usual. However you choose to remember that day, I hope you'll take a moment and remember Jesus' story, because I think it is a wonderful blessing that his story of lost-ness and our own story of loss are linked now.

Jesus talks a lot about carrying your cross and suffering for his name's sake and other such things that sound awkward to our modern sensibilities, and we tend to separate the harshness of those kinds of words from the softer texture of these parables about a lost sheep and a lost coin. But the truth is they go together. Jesus carried a perspective that is only possible when you are brushed up face to face with the reality of pain, the reality of evil, the reality of reality. Jesus spoke as one who knew what this dusty road to Lost looked like. And he won't let us forget it.

A lot of times it made him say things that are hard for us to stomach. If we read it as we should, probably all of it is prone to give us heartburn. But Jesus also said some beautiful things—in fact, some of the most beautiful things ever said. Not because they are more eloquent than Shakespeare or as packed with meaning as Tolstoy or as melodic as Maya Angelou—they are beautiful because they were spoken by one who knew how lost we all were, and still stuck around. One who knew how hard it was to hold on to each other when the world seemed to be tearing itself apart, but held on just the same.

The truth is we're all lost, no matter how good we are at faking it. There is no GPS, no on-board navigation system that can bring us back as long as we are determined to set the course. Our faith is not just a set of beliefs or a set of behaviors, but an encounter with the One who has dropped everything to come and find us. The One who stays up all night, searching through the rubble and the dust of our lives, hoping to find our hearts. The One who loves us irresponsibly, with a love that doesn't make sense and doesn't follow the rules. The One who calls on us to share that same irresponsible love with the folks on the edges. To believe in our own acceptance so that we might believe that they are just as acceptable in the sight of God.

Hold on to these stories. Because they are not so much about what it's like being lost—God knows we don't need any lessons about that—no, these stories are about the business of being found. And the joy of finding. They are a promise to all of us who find ourselves parched and empty on the road without a name or destination, whether we've admitted to ourselves our lost-ness or we're still pretending to know what the heck we're doing out here. These stories are a promise that there is another one out here with us, hidden by the dust and the darkness, who is looking. Who looks like a shepherd, or a woman who's lost her coin, or a volunteer in a pile of rubble. Keep searching. Keep living out of the hope that we are all on the way to being found, for there is One who will take our hand, ready or not, and lead us back. Back to home. Back to God. Back to each other.

36 What Comes Between

In the morning Jonathan went out into the field to the appoint-ment with David, and with him was a little boy. He said to the boy, "Run and find the arrows that I shoot." As the boy ran, he shot an arrow beyond him. When the boy came to the place where Jonathan's arrow had fallen, Jonathan called after the boy and said, "Is the arrow not beyond you?" Jonathan called after the boy, "Hurry, be quick, do not linger." So Jonathan's boy gathered up the arrows and came to his master. But the boy knew nothing; only Jonathan and David knew the arrangement. Jonathan gave his weapons to the boy and said to him, "Go and carry them to the city." As soon as the boy had gone, David rose from beside the stone heap and prostrated himself with his face to the ground. He bowed three times, and they kissed each other, and wept with each other; David wept the more. Then Jonathan said to David, "Go in peace, since both of us have sworn in the name of the LORD, saying, 'The LORD shall be between me and you, and between my descendants and your descendants, forever.'" He got up and left; and Jonathan went into the city. (1 Samuel 20:35–42)

In the little place I used to work, the Yeilding Chapel at Birmingham-Southern College, everything is round. The walls are round, the altar is round, the original pulpit is round—if it can be round, it is.

And one of the most interesting things about that very round place is that the altar is smack dab in the middle of the room. Since there is not really a front or a back to the sanctuary, that is the only place it can be, right in the middle of everything that's going on. And that takes a little getting used to if you're accustomed to sitting in rows facing the front.

At the same time, my favorite thing about that sanctuary is the very awkwardness of it. With the altar being in the center, and all the pews wrapping around it, you cannot look at the altar or see the cross without also seeing the people on the other side of the sanctuary. There is nowhere you can sit in that place that you don't always see both the altar and the other folks who have gathered to worship. And maybe, despite all its awkwardness, that's the way it should be, that whenever we look for God, we find each other, and vice versa—even when that's not what we started out to do. The architecture gently reminds us that God is not just at the beginning or the end, but always smack dab in the middle of our lives.

There was an ancient Christian named Dorotheos of Gaza, whose wisdom was so renowned that folks used to come to him with all kinds of questions. And when one of his students asked him to describe his understanding of the universe, Dorotheos answered him by drawing a great circle—a giant circle of humanity. Standing at the edge of the circle, every last human being was facing the center and joining hands with those on their left and right. And in the center of the circle was God, so that as each human took a step toward the center, toward God, they were also making their way toward one another. And whenever they came closer to one another, they also discovered they were coming closer to God.

For those of us on the edge facing in, we all must walk a different direction in order to get from where we are to the center. If we all were to walk the same way, only a handful of us would ever reach God. But if we each find our own way to move toward the middle, walking ever closer to each other, we will eventually find ourselves there in the middle of everything, in the presence of our Creator. If I meet someone who seems very different from me, who believes different things and whose skin is different and whose story is different and nothing at all seems the same about the two of us, there is still one thing that will be the same about us in the end: the God who called us both, and who waits for both of us at the end of these different roads.

Now that sort of thinking can be fairly troublesome for us Christians, because even though we tell ourselves we've been freed from the burden of the law and all those strange commandments in Leviticus, we still want to follow the rules. We love rules, because they give us some direction. They tell us which way is up and which way is down. They tell us who is in and who is out. They keep us safe because they keep us the same.

And most of the time we use the Bible not as a door, but as a fence—keeping those who don't look like us or act like us on the other side. Chances are, with a few exceptions, the people in your church for the most part look and act like you. The neighbors on your street look and act a lot like you. It's just easier to be around people that are the same. Our great-grandfathers and great-grandmothers thought it just didn't make sense to have white people and black people in the same church. After all, they couldn't shop in the same stores or use the same water fountains; why share a church? And as much as we want to judge them for their mistakes, most of the time it doesn't seem as if we're doing very much to find a solution. The Christian faith is a wonderful thing, but just like anything else, if manipulated enough, it can be used to justify horrible things like racism and classism and war and greed. Someone has said the Bible is like nitroglycerine: you can use it to build bombs or you can use it to prevent heart attacks.

Besides, we've come so far in breaking down those boundaries. Maybe you've heard these voices in your church: *We've moved on from those days of all-out classism and separation. We know what it means to be the Body of Christ, don't we? We know how to care for our brothers and sisters, right? People can come to our churches if they want. It's not like we're barring the doors. If Hispanics want to come to our church, they're more than welcome. They might not understand any of what we say, but they're welcome to sit in the pews like the rest of us. If the poor and homeless want to come and worship with us, that's fine, as long as they don't go around begging during the church service. After all, we have to have some order here. It is church. If a homosexual couple wants to worship with us, well, I guess that's okay, too. As long as they know they are sinners and we absolutely disagree with who they are and the way they're living their lives, of course they're welcome.*

I'm not telling you what to believe as an individual. I'm talking about what happens when we come together. When we are the Church. When we are the Body of Christ. We are always talking about having God in our relationships, but usually we are talking about how to have better relationships with those who are already our friends. What does it mean to really have God at the center of *all* our relationships?

There once was a gentleman named Saul who, by no fault of his own, was elected the first president of Israel, even though he wasn't really running. In fact, he was so unsettled by the prospect of this new responsibility that when it came time to crown him, they found him hiding under his luggage. And for some mysterious reason, this does not lead the folks who find him cowering there under his carry-on to reconsider their decision. Well, after a few years, like most people in power, Saul grows to like the position. Truth be told, he starts to covet it.

That's where our old friend David comes into the picture. As you might remember, even though David is just a kid, he walks onto the battlefield with a measly little slingshot and when he walks off the field, there is one less Philistine giant. So naturally, David's PR ratings just shoot through the roof. The people love him. And unfortunately, Saul is so jealous that he doesn't realize the people can love David *and* still love him, too. Primarily, Saul is concerned that when he dies, they won't make his son Jonathan king, they will crown David instead.

In the meantime, David and Jonathan become best friends. The Bible says it better than I ever could: "Jonathan loved him as his own soul." Despite their different backgrounds, their very different families (David's dad manages sheep all day and Jonathan's is a king), there is something amazing between the two of them that draws them together.

But Saul continues to grow in hatred for David, attempting unsuccessfully to kill him several times. Finally, David comes to

Jonathan and says, "Your dad is trying to kill me, you've got to help me." And Jonathan, wanting to protect his friend and still loving his father, is stuck between his love for a friend and a son's love for his father. He must choose between his dad, the man who gave him life and a home and a future, and this unlikely friend of his. And he decides, against all practical judgment, to protect his friend. In tears, Jonathan helps David escape and, in doing so, gives up on his chance to be king. In that moment, when he has turned his back on his own future to show love for his friend, Jonathan utters some prophetic words: "Our friendship runs deeper than blood, is bigger than any promise we could make to each other, because it is the Lord that is between us."

At some point we as Christians have to decide what it is that we are willing to let stand in the way of our being together. It is one thing to fight and disagree and have conflict—that is a normal part of healthy living. But to shut out people in Christ's name is another thing altogether. The day the church fails to bless human relationships, fails to welcome all people, as broken and bruised as they may be, is the day that the church forgets the awesome responsibility left on its shoulders. If we are going to divide up the Body of Christ over any disagreement we might have, then we have forgotten who we are. Whose name we claim to live under. Who it is at the center of our circle, at the altar of our hearts, beckoning us all to move closer to one another, in spite of (and in celebration of) all these differences. Jonathan had it right—"The Lord is between us. It doesn't so much matter what stands in our way if that is the center of who we are together."

At some point, we have to realize that our calling is not toward the sky, not toward heaven; it is toward each other. And no matter how we get there, no matter how different we are when we arrive, we will know that the only thing standing between me and you and all the rest of us is the Lord. The Lord is between us.

37 The Sinai School of Career Development

"The cry of the Israelites has now come to me; I have also seen how the Egyptians oppress them. So come, I will send you to Pharaoh to bring my people, the Israelites, out of Egypt." But Moses said to God, "Who am I that I should go to Pharaoh, and bring the Israelites out of Egypt?" He said, "I will be with you; and this shall be the sign for you that it is I who sent you: when you have brought the people out of Egypt, you shall worship God on this mountain." (Exodus 3:9–12)

If I have to boil down everything I have to say into one sermon, it would be a sermon on vocation. Not the kind of vocation you study on "Career Day" in high school. Not the kind of vocation you apply for at the Human Resources department, though those things are a part of it. The vocation I'm interested in comes from the same root word as *vocal*, and it means our calling—what and who we are called by God to be.

My faith journey has been wrapped up in trying to figure out who the heck I was and what it was I was supposed to be doing. It's still about that. In fact, I think if you had to sum up the Bible in just one theme, it would be about humanity searching for who it is trying to be, in light of God's love. Unfortunately, it is a lot

173

easier to get a driver's license or a Social Security card than it is to figure out who you are. Believe it or not, it's tougher to find your vocation than it is to find a job. It is a lot easier to assume you know what and who you are than to actually chase down the mystery inside you.

Which brings me to Moses. A nice enough fellow, I guess. Spared from death by a wise mother and an improvised wicker life raft, raised as the adopted grandson of the same man who killed all the other male Hebrew babies, he is now hiding with his wife in the mountains, trying to make an honest living looking after his father-in-law's flocks, and escaping the guilt he brought on himself by murdering an Egyptian slave master. He's done a pretty good job of making his own life. He's made some poor decisions, but things have turned out pretty well: a quiet, respectable living, good family, nice place in the suburbs, far from the rough injustice that he's seen too much of. The roller coaster has leveled off. He has his AARP card. He's done growing up, as far as he's concerned.

But one day, Moses doesn't pay attention to where he's going. He's not all that good at watching sheep, if you must know. Most of the time the sheep herd him. Anyway, he somehow ends up on top of Mount Sinai. A holy mountain, whatever that means. And there, where the air is a bit thinner and everything down below seems much smaller, he thinks he sees something. *Surely that's not what I think it is.* But then he sees it again. *I've been spending too much time with sheep.* But then there was no mistaking what it was or what he heard: his own name.

It may be the best thing in the world when someone knows your name. Not just how to spell it or how to pronounce it right, but they know it because *they know you.* Those folks tend to say your name a little differently—our families, our best friends, the people who know us best. When we hear it, we know immediately that we are loved, that we belong, that we have a reason to be. If you can imagine getting all the people who love you like that into one room, having them all call your name at the same time, I think you might have some idea of what this was like for Moses. It is the voice that tugs at our hearts in our happiest and most frustrating and most confusing and most brilliant moments—the voice that whispers who we were made to be. Not necessarily who we want to be all the time. Not necessarily the direction we would choose for ourselves. And it's not necessarily the clearest of voices, for that matter, or the most comforting. Most of us, instead of having a burning bush tell us where to go, end up *feeling* like a burning bush. As if there should be nothing left of us, but somehow there still is.

While stories like this inspire us, they are also limiting because they are not our own, and we read them looking for the wrong clues. We are left wondering why the bushes in our lives never catch fire, or when the issues of our day will become so crystal clear that we will have no choice but to respond.

While in college, I traveled with a service-learning class to Calcutta, trying to learn what it was that made Mother Teresa do what she did. All being well-schooled in stories like Moses', we had left our little school fully expecting that the bushes in India would be much more flammable.

Every morning we marched down the broken sidewalks, stepping over the dying, trying to get to the hospice where we would help the dying. We spent our days bathing, feeding, and tending to the needs of broken bodies whose language sounded like nonsense in our ears. This meant that our ability to care for them was limited to our ability to guess their needs, which we quickly discovered was not a gift any one of us possessed. At best, we were in the way. Recalling the expectations and good wishes of all those who had sent me, I thought of all the money, the preparation, and time spent to bring me to this moment of utter uselessness.

One frustrated night, I wandered my way into evening prayers, looking for a breath of familiarity in what seemed a suffocating sea of difference. I hoped God had survived the journey intact. Having visited a few of Mother Teresa's other homes, I immediately recognized the décor. All of her chapels are the same: neutral walls holding small depictions of the Stations of the Cross, a simple table for an altar, and a large wooden crucifix hanging next to some of Christ's last words, "I thirst." The two words are in black capital letters, and are easily the most striking feature of the room, though the choice to include them, all by themselves, seemed a bit random to me.

I knew we would begin the prayers in silence, and I had been coveting that coming quiet all afternoon. The noise had just become too much for me, as polluted as the air and just as stifling. I needed a moment apart, to reflect, to gather my thoughts. I was convinced that if I could just turn off the world for a moment, where it was just me and God, I could get my bearings again.

But there is no silence in Calcutta. I'm not sure what I was imagining would happen, but the city was not going to observe evening prayers, and outside the open windows, life very much went on. The sounds of the cars and the arguments and the scavenging birds and the distorted amplifications of the corner mosque—all of it seemed to poison my moment with God. Wanting to leave, I scanned the room for an easy exit, and found my eyes landing instead on those large black letters on the wall. I THIRST.

And for a brief moment, life broke through. These two little words, a drop out of the Bible's sea, were meant to serve as a translation for those of us who could not yet speak the language. The sounds of the world that broke through the walls and windows were not a distraction to prayer, they were the very reason for it. What I heard as chaos and brokenness and cacophony was God's pain as much as it was anyone else's, a summons to service. Distorted and unintelligible like the Muslim cantor's calling, but a calling all the same. And so that night, for the first time, I prayed myself *into* the world rather than out of it.

For Moses and the rest of us, responding to God's call is not a one-time decision. It demands a lifetime of fragile moments where we discover what our souls are made of—where we choose, sometimes unknowingly, to be the agents of something greater than ourselves. To gape in awe at the simultaneous beauty and tragedy of the world around us, only to discover our feet moving in response to what we have seen.

And so there on top of that mountain, the same place where he will receive the Ten Commandments and meet God again, Moses finds the strangest character of all: himself. Not that he suddenly has any answers. He is afraid and uncertain and confused, maybe now more than ever, and he certainly has a long way to go, but at least he has a direction. He asks God for a business card, and God only answers, "I am who I am." As if to say, "From here on out, there are no permanent answers in this business of faith, only clues." Otherwise we might be tricked into thinking this was a science and not an art.

So here's an invitation. On the days when you feel most out of touch, when the canvas is blank and everything is possible, spend some time listening. Not just in the quiet and obvious places, but in all places. Because you never know when you'll hear your own name, spoken by the voice that knows you better than you know yourself. Calling you to be the most frightening thing of all—yourself.

38 The Awful Quiet

Then Job answered: "Today also my complaint is bitter; his hand is heavy despite my groaning. Oh, that I knew where I might find him, that I might come even to his dwelling! I would lay my case before him, and fill my mouth with arguments. I would learn what he would answer me, and understand what he would say to me. Would he contend with me in the greatness of his power? No; but he would give heed to me. There an upright person could reason with him, and I should be acquitted forever by my judge. If I go forward, he is not there; or backward, I cannot perceive him; on the left he hides, and I cannot behold him; I turn to the right, but I cannot see him. . . . God has made my heart faint; the Almighty has terrified me; If only I could vanish in darkness, and thick darkness would cover my face!" (Job 23:1–9, 16–17)

My God, my God, why have you forsaken me? (Psalm 22:1)

Indeed, the word of God is living and active, sharper than any two-edged sword, piercing until it divides soul from spirit, joints from marrow; it is able to judge the thoughts and intentions of the heart. (Hebrews 4:12)

There was a time not so long ago when it was possible to be quiet. To sit in silence. I'm not so sure that's the case anymore. I don't think many people like silence. Our kids or our kids' kids will read one day in a history book about a world without cell phones. When people had unexpressed thoughts. A world before e-mail, where it actually took a bit of effort to say something to someone else.

But as it stands, as communication becomes easier and easier, something worth saying seems to be harder to find. We keep up the noise, though, because we are more comfortable with distractions than we are with the silence. We turn the TV on and get through our days, not expecting to learn anything, not expecting any transformation, just hoping to be numbed long enough to not notice the time passing.

The truth be told, a lot of us, including myself, are just plain afraid of the quiet. Silence means something is broken, the power is out, nobody needs me. Noise and conversation—these things mean that I am important. I am valuable. As embarrassing as it is for the rest of us when someone's cell phone or pager goes off during a play or a movie or a worship service, it does send a clear message: I am important. People need my immediate attention so much that they cannot wait to talk to me. And that's a good feeling.

It's not any different with our spiritual lives. We want to feel as if there is spiritual noise in our lives. And that is why these texts are so frightening to me. These are the type of scripture passages that when it comes time to say, "Thanks be to God," you're not so sure if you mean it. In the Old Testament passage cited here, Job has lost his home, his worldly possessions, his family, and his health. But it's not those things that really upset him. His pain comes because, in the middle of his crisis, God has suddenly cut off all lines of communication, and Job just needs God to say something. Anything. Job has been handed every suffering in the book, but the one that hurts most is God's quiet.

Using a different tactic, the Psalmist tries to remind God of the great things he has done in the past, in the hopes that it will inspire God to do something again. It's almost as if he's trying to remind God how God is supposed to act, spelling out a divine job description. And these words are made even more powerful a few hundred years after they are written, when Jesus speaks them as he hangs on a cross, experiencing maybe for the first time what it is like to hear the silence of God. And it even frightens Jesus. Just say something. *Anything.* But don't be so quiet.

I would venture a guess that everyone has felt that stillness. That uncertainty. What am I supposed to do with myself? Who am I supposed to be? What do you want from me? Feeling as if you have said *your* part of the conversation, now why won't God just respond? Why won't God give me answers? There is not a louder sound in the world than God's silence. So when the letter to the Hebrews talks about the way God's word divides soul from spirit, joints from marrow, we know that it is not only God's *word* that has that immeasurable power—God's silence is just as potent.

Some of us just give up on God when God doesn't talk back. If he isn't willing to talk, I'm not willing to listen. And we walk away from God and faith and all those things that have become so painful. There are many people for whom God is very real, but God is so quiet they would rather not even bother. Some of us decide that after reading the Bible, and seeing all these faithful persons who get to share God's fellowship, God's silence must simply mean we are not wanted. God doesn't want what we have. And some of us, when faced with the quiet of God, fill up the void with our own noise. We claim every voice we hear is the voice of God, and every decision we make is the will of God. Our ears are so sore from listening to the silence that we just give up listening and start speaking for God. Some Christian worship, I daresay, is just a thin cover for a bunch of people who are too afraid to admit that God has been too quiet as of late.

But as much as we might want God to do something flashy and bold and clear in our lives, I'm not so sure that's the way God has ever worked. God doesn't sit us down and feed us a meal that will end our hunger forever—most of the time our experiences of God leave us hungrier than we were when we sat down. Every revelation is a small piece of a huge puzzle we won't fully understand for a long, long time.

And I'm not sure we would know what to make of God when God does choose to speak unless we first know what it is like to stand there in the quiet. There is something powerful in the silence. After all, the most intimate relationships in life are not necessarily the ones you can keep up a conversation with, but the ones you can sit for hours in silence with and not feel a bit strange. Sometimes it is enough just to be in the presence of God and not have a word spoken.

As much as I would like to be able to create instant fire, or invoke the voice of James Earl Jones to speak to you out of some storm cloud, that is not the way hope or love or faith work. As hard as it is to stand in the stillness, hearing only the echoes of your own voice reverberate, that is the place where the amazing really happens. The German theologian Jürgen Moltmann once said, "It is when Jesus falls silent on the cross that he speaks to us with the greatest intensity." We gather together around that cross, where God fell silent. But we gather in the hope that the silence is not the end of things. It is only the beginning. And even as we wait here, hungry for something to hear, the silence is not empty. We are not alone. We are held in a love more profound than words can speak, more profound than any one sign or revelation could teach us. The quietness of God does not mean that we have been forgotten—instead it speaks volumes about the love of a God who stands with us in our silence, holding us, waiting with us, loving us even now.

39 Waiting by the Side of the Road

They came to Jericho. As he and his disciples and a large crowd were leaving Jericho, Bartimaeus son of Timaeus, a blind beggar, was sitting by the roadside. When he heard that it was Jesus of Nazareth, he began to shout out and say, "Jesus, Son of David, have mercy on me!" Many sternly ordered him to be quiet, but he cried out even more loudly, "Son of David, have mercy on me!" Jesus stood still and said, "Call him here." And they called the blind man, saying to him, "Take heart; get up, he is calling you." So throwing off his cloak, he sprang up and came to Jesus. Then Jesus said to him, "What do you want me to do for you?" The blind man said to him, "My teacher, let me see again." Jesus said to him, "Go; your faith has made you well." Immediately he regained his sight and followed him on the way. (Mark 10:46–52)

Waiting is not an easy thing to do. If we had the choice, most of us would avoid it altogether. After all, we like things *here*. Now. Not almost here or not quite yet. We want things to happen immediately. And it's not just the little things, either. Look in the paper or watch the evening news—they are both filled with stories of women and men who get so caught up in getting what they want immediately that they do the unthinkable.

But there is no getting around time. We can't change its speed. We would like to pretend sometimes that all the planning and the streamlining and the organization might make a dent in it, but time doesn't flinch. We still have to wait, even when the waiting seems to be a waste of time.

Whoever it was that penned the Gospel of Mark, he shared our dislike for waiting. Maybe he was in a hurry to get his story finished, because it is the shortest of the four by far. He doesn't have very good grammar, he doesn't use nice literary transitions like the other three, he doesn't write in poetic language. Jesus does everything "immediately." In fact, "immediately" may be Mark's favorite word, occurring twenty-seven times in just sixteen chapters. Mark doesn't tell us where or how Jesus was born, and he abruptly ends his Gospel with an empty tomb.

And if all that wasn't enough, Jesus acts a bit strange in Mark. Throughout the story, Jesus repeatedly tells everyone around him to keep his identity a secret.

Which is not hard. Most people, even those who spend the most time around Jesus, are pretty much in the dark all the time. People are drawn to his miracles, fascinated by his teachings; they desperately long for his healing power, but they still don't quite seem to get it. Most of them don't seem to have a clue about who he is. Mark wants us readers to know that it is not a given that you will recognize Jesus when he comes walking down Main Street of your hometown. The teachers and scribes who spent night and day reading scripture and talking about it, the very ones who had devoted their lives to finding God, looked at Jesus and could only see a threat. Those who had friends and family who were sick or dying, the ones who strangely were able to believe that Jesus might be able to help them, looked at him and only saw a mysterious albeit talented doc-in-the-box. Even the disciples, the motley crew that Jesus had handpicked to follow him around, even granting them the ability to perform their own miracles, can't readily see Jesus for who he is. They take half the book—eight chapters— before speak-before-you-think Peter blurts out that Jesus is the Messiah.

None of these could see. In fact, in Mark's Gospel at least, it is only the sick and the suffering who are able to see Jesus for who he really is. And Bartimaeus is no different. Probably the victim of conjunctivitis, he has lost his sight, and he has been waiting here by the side of this road. To the busy people who pass him every day, making their way to work or class, he just seems like an odd old man. Lazy. Confused. A pitiable and awkward waste of life. Few people stop to talk anymore, but he has been out here so long he is like a fixture there on the curb. Minutes and hours and days and years pass, and he is still just there, trapped in his own darkness. Maybe people stop occasionally to give him some of their excess, hoping to make themselves feel a bit better in the process, but secretly they wonder why he remains. What does he have to wait for? Behind it all, while he passes the time humming with the birds or tracing lines in the sand or talking to himself, *he is waiting*.

And to those of us who walk by him, it is hard to know what he is waiting for. What hope could this blind old fool possibly have? He is probably crazy. Most of us have become so accustomed to our own blindness we have stopped believing there might be an end to it, so it is really hard to imagine what keeps this man going other than insanity. "There is no reason to have hope!" we want to shout at him, shout at ourselves. There is no medical treatment for his condition, there is no place for him to go other than this dusty road outside Jericho. But he just sits there, waiting. Hoping for the impossible.

And one day, the Impossible comes walking down the road. It is not so obvious that the others would notice. There are no fire-works. There are no clearly marked signs. No one had it recorded in their day planners. His name is Jesus, a name like any other, from Nazareth, a place like any other. So when Bartimaeus stands up and starts shouting at him, even calling him the Son of King David, well, that is just too much. We are kind enough to let this guy stay here all the time, but this is inappropriate. "Show some self-control," more than a few people loudly whisper. But Bartimaeus cannot be still. He is not like these others, because you see, *he has been waiting*. Waiting for a man he did not know, for a God he could not see. And now that he has found him, Bartimaeus cannot be still.

And Jesus, too, has been waiting. Waiting for the next one who would recognize him without proof, without evidence, without reason for hope. "Take heart—cheer up," the crowd politely says to Bartimaeus when Jesus calls for him, and the irony is that Bartimaeus is the person there who least needs that advice. Maybe this is why Jesus spends so much energy being secretive, so that he can find those who have been long expecting him. And there, on that dusty and unimportant road outside Jericho, Jesus finds another one. "You've found me," he says. "What is it that you have been waiting for?"

"Let me see again," Bartimaeus whispers or laughs or cries, we don't know. What we do know is that the impossible happened that day. The crowd gathered for a show. They were hoping for something notable. Worth their while. And while they got to see a man healed of his blindness, they missed the biggest miracle of all, standing there right in front of them. And one short week later, some of these same people would gather to kill him on top of a garbage heap outside Golgotha. Only the one who was waiting, hoping, searching—only the one who had expected the unexpected recognized this man—this Jesus—this nobody—as a Savior.

So, like Bartimaeus, we stand here on the side of this road, waiting for a stranger. We do not know what to expect, what to look for, what we will hear, what we will see on the other side of all this waiting, but we trust that when the Impossible comes our way, we will know it, and we will have the courage to stand up and call his name into the darkness. To proclaim him as our Messiah. The one who has come to heal us.

But until then, we must wait. There will be doubt that feels inescapable. Fear that won't go away, fear that sometimes overshadows even the brightest of our hopes and dreams. But faith calls us to remain. It is the thing that tells us against all good reason that there is something worth waiting for. Faith is the hunger that keeps us in the waiting room of our lives, hoping against hope for good news. Faith is the something that tells us that if we wait here with Bartimaeus long enough, someone will come for us to make us see again. Maybe long after we have given up hope, someone will come for us to do the impossible. Maybe long after our lives seem to fall short of our dreams, someone will come for us to give his life so that we might have life again. Someone will come for us. And we will be here, waiting.

40 Stranger in the Shadows

Then Joseph could no longer control himself before all those who stood by him, and he cried out, "Send everyone away from me." So no one stayed with him when Joseph made himself known to his brothers. And he wept so loudly that the Egyptians heard it, and the household of Pharaoh heard it. Joseph said to his brothers, "I am Joseph. Is my father still alive?" But his brothers could not answer him, so dismayed were they at his presence. Then Joseph said to his brothers, "Come closer to me." And they came closer. He said, "I am your brother, Joseph, whom you sold into Egypt. And now do not be distressed, or angry with yourselves, because you sold me here; for God sent me before you to preserve life. For the famine has been in the land these two years; and there are five more years in which there will be neither plowing nor harvest. God sent me before you to preserve for you a remnant on earth, and to keep alive for you many survivors. So it was not you who sent me here, but God; he has made me a father to Pharaoh, and lord of all his house and ruler over all the land of Egypt. Hurry and go up to my father and say to him, 'Thus says your son Joseph, God has made me lord of all Egypt; come down to me, do not delay. You shall settle in the land of Goshen, and you shall be near me, you and your children and your children's children, as well as your flocks, your herds, and all that you have. I will provide for you

there—since there are five more years of famine to come—so that you and your household, and all that you have, will not come to poverty.' And now your eyes and the eyes of my brother Benjamin see that it is my own mouth that speaks to you. You must tell my father how greatly I am honored in Egypt, and all that you have seen. Hurry and bring my father down here." Then he fell upon his brother Benjamin's neck and wept, while Benjamin wept upon his neck. And he kissed all his brothers and wept upon them; and after that his brothers talked with him.
(Genesis 45:1–15)

There are always two stories being told in the Genesis text, parallel, but quite different. One of hope and promise and God, and another of pain and mistrust and shadow. A family therapist would have her hands full sorting through the many betrayals, misunderstandings, and abuses that color the pages of this first book of the Bible. Stories like Adam and Eve's disobedience, God's destructive flood, Noah and his sons, Cain and Abel, Abraham and Isaac, Sara and Hagar, Jacob and Esau—the list goes on and on. The point is that they all hint at the same central idea: sometimes it is the very relationships in which we should feel the safest that we are the most vulnerable. And so it is fitting that the Genesis story leaves us, in the end, with this character Joseph. Weeping.

The Joseph story is one of the more popular Old Testament stories because it can so easily be translated into the language of coloring books and cut-out paper dolls. The biggest prerequisite for any such story is a happy ending, where the good boy or girl receives the blessings of God and all the players exit off the stage with no hard feelings. And it is in precisely that moment that the lectionary leaves us, with an almost superhuman Joseph who bursts into tears and forgives his brothers. The message seems simple enough for those of us who want some practical morality we can take with us from each Bible story: Forgive each other like Joseph. And maybe if we just read this passage in isolation we could do that, but we don't, so we can't. Joseph's tears tug us into a deeper participation in the text, calling us to hear this particular story as a piece of a larger epic. That is certainly what Joseph and his brothers are doing in this place. There is a sense for all of them that they are standing at the intersection of their very lives—that strange

moment, one of only a few in every life, where the past and pres-
ent collide like awkward strangers who are forced to introduce
themselves.

We have to remember that Joseph still remembers. The earthy
walls and floor still damp from the last rain. Standing there naked,
having been violently stripped of his cloak just moments before by
his brothers. His brothers, who laughed and mocked and smiled
with that teeth-grinding envy Joseph had never seen before, but
would see much more of in his lifetime. And as he stands there,
deep in that shadowy pit, his feet suctioned to the sticky muck
beneath him, he feels a lump form in his throat. A lump of regret,
of deep hurt, of loneliness—it is a staggering new emotion for this
17-year-old who has been pampered and doted upon from the day
of his birth. And standing there, shivering in the shadows, picking
up unintelligible words from his brothers' argument up above, the
lump swells until he cannot swallow. He isn't sure if he wants to
cry or scream so he does neither, and as they lift him back out of
the pit and into the hands of a stranger, he searches their faces for
an explanation, one last attempt to make sense out of this sudden
chaos. But, of course, it does not make sense. And as Joseph is
bound like a criminal and carried off to a foreign land where his
language is not spoken and his father is not known and his God is
not worshiped, his innocence is left behind, in the shadows of that
pit. With every rickety thump-thump-thump of the wheels against
the desert floor, Joseph finds himself farther and farther away from
understanding what his brothers have done.

Every human life spends some time in that place, the shadowy
hole Joseph found himself in through no action of his own. Not to
say Joseph hadn't indirectly asked for it—we have all been around
those people who are so sure God has something to do with their
lives that we cannot be around them without shuddering—partly
because we disapprove of their arrogance, but maybe more so
because they speak to our own insecurities about God and ourselves. And Joseph is certainly one of those people, someone who
could benefit from one of those Dale Carnegie courses where they
teach you to watch what you say in certain social circles. The
youngest son and brother, walking around, spouting off his supe-
rior future to everyone else, as if they will be just as excited as he

is. And when Dad returns home from his big trip, with trinkets for eleven and a shiny new Beer-sheba Braves jacket for Joseph, well, that was the last straw. It didn't help when he wouldn't take the fool thing off, either. He wore it to school, out in the fields, there was that time Judah caught him wearing it under the covers in the bunk bed—just pouring salt into the wound. The kid took it too far.

But by no fault of his own, mind you. He was just proud. Proud of who he was and who he had come from. That jacket spoke something of that, so when they tore it off his back, Joseph saw something very different from what his brothers saw. His brothers could only see their resentment and bitter jealousy. All Joseph could see was his very identity, his connectedness to his father and family, being ripped from him. And that's why, beginning with that shadowy pit and rickety old slave cart, things were going to change. He was never, ever, ever going to let the world hurt him like that again. Up until that point, he had not known that other people were capable of such cruelty, but from that moment on, he told himself he would never forget it.

Something profound happens when you swallow a worldview like that. It is something akin to looking at the other half of a picture that you thought you knew well and discovering something altogether new and unsettling. At some point you begin to tell yourself that this new discomforting discovery is the truth of the thing. That you were blind, stupid, immature before, but now that you are bitter, you really know something. You understand reality. You can appreciate the way things work. And so you set to work creating a life for yourself free from vulnerability, free from needing anyone else, choosing instead to remain in the shadows.

I grew up loving my father with what I can only call my whole heart. He was my hero, my role model, my companion, all rolled into one. One of the first things I used to do with any of my new friends was introduce them to my dad, because I wanted them to know me by knowing him. I could not have been prouder of who he was, or how he loved me. No one but my father could make me laugh until I cried. My relationship with my father was off-limits to the chaos and confusion that visited the other parts of my life every so often. But, of course, that wasn't true, and when my mother tearfully told me of their impending separation, a lump formed in my throat.

I found myself in that same pit Joseph did—betrayed not by any one person, but by the very life I had bought into. Suddenly I was trapped between two very different stories: one of the father I had grown up with and another, dissonant story that seemed to negate the first. Over the course of the next several weeks, I fully accepted this new truth I had found. That people were not faithful, that promises were not kept, that love was just some temporary barrier to chaos and shadow. I was not a pleasant person to be around, but worse than that, I couldn't see what I was doing to myself. Long after my parents had reconciled their marriage, I still lurked in the shadows, unwilling to believe that anything good was true.

And it is with the same grinding teeth that Joseph holds onto his bitterness, running his brothers through an emotional spin-cycle, exercising the full range of his new power. For now, they are the ones trapped in the shadows of a pit: faced with a famine, a lonely father whose unhappiness they have contributed to in no small degree, and now this overeager state employee who seems determined to break them. Accused of being liars, spies, and thieves, they are certain that their misfortune is the product of bad karma. And they are not far from the truth. Standing there above his brothers, their feet slowly sinking into the muck, Joseph is in control.

For a long time I didn't speak to my father, and if I did, it was in short, melodramatic phrases, an angry teenager's specialty. He tried in every way he knew how to show me that he was painfully sorry, and for a while I mistook that relationship I had with him as one of power, that somehow I could turn the tide on him and make him feel as empty as he had made me feel. And it is strange to me now, but in some sense I lost God when I could not embrace my father. The God I grew up with—the God of Sunday school—handed out blessings to those he loved. That is a great story if you are feeling particularly favored, but it is made of very different stuff when you hear it from a pit.

But then one afternoon, for no apparent reason, I let my guard down. Only for a moment. And my father made me laugh again. And what began as a tiny fissure in some great wall soon gave way to a flood of emotion. Suddenly, I had my story back. And this man, shadows and all, was my father. The same one who had coached my little league teams, rushed me to the hospital for stitches, and loved me still. And I found that, despite my anger, despite my deep hurt, no matter how much I didn't want it to be true, I still loved him as much or more than I ever had. This new, discomforting view of the picture was not the entire frame, but only a small piece of a larger puzzle. And when I swallowed that, as hard as it was, I got my father back. Maybe more important, I got myself back, and I got God back.

I had been looking for God in my parent's separation—trying to find out why God had done this to me. But I was simply looking in the wrong place. My pain was the product of people, finite, confused people just like you and me. It wasn't until I looked back that I could see the God who had been patiently waiting with me in my pain.

So there Joseph stands, in that space between the darkness of the past and the faces of his brothers—and for just a moment—just a split second—he peers out across the gap of these many years of separation to the faces of these, his brothers.

And he weeps.

He weeps for that 17-year-old scared in the pit. He weeps for the lonely nights when he had wished for the company of his family. He weeps for the joy of seeing his own flesh and bone there before him. He weeps because he can no longer deny his connection, his love for them, no matter how little sense it makes. And maybe most importantly, he weeps for something the others cannot see. In stepping out of the shadows, Joseph is able to see for the first time that his story is more than a string of misfortunes. In every act of moral depravity committed against him, there was another face with him in the shadows. He weeps for the God he was afraid to see until now, stitched into the very fabric of his story.

For the first time since he stood in the pit, Joseph stops trying to make sense of what has happened. Because what he needed, after all is said and done, was not an explanation or an apology, though those things are certainly important. What he needed most of all was for it to mean something. And there, standing in the embrace of his rediscovered family, Joseph can claim that meaning.

Working even in a world filled with human mistake and greed and misunderstanding, God kept good on promises made.

And maybe that is the biggest difference between us and these characters in the pages of Genesis. It's not that God speaks to them directly, or gives them descendants like dust, or helps them interpret important people's dreams; none of that seems as important or convincing to them as we might think. No, what separates us from them is that, at the core of who they are, in the very depths of their souls, they realize that God is there. Quiet, but there. Lurking in the shadows of all their pitfalls, gently nudging them— and us—to the tears of reconciliation.

 # 41 What to Say at the End

When they came to the place that is called The Skull, they cruci-
fied Jesus there with the criminals, one on his right and one on his
left. Then Jesus said, "Father, forgive them; for they do not know
what they are doing." And they cast lots to divide his clothing.
And the people stood by, watching; but the leaders scoffed at him,
saying, "He saved others; let him save himself if he is the Messiah
of God, his chosen one!" The soldiers also mocked him, coming up
and offering him sour wine, and saying, "If you are the King of
the Jews, save yourself!" There was also an inscription over him,
"This is the King of the Jews." One of the criminals who were
hanged there kept deriding him and saying, "Are you not the
Messiah? Save yourself and us!" But the other rebuked him, saying,
"Do you not fear God, since you are under the same sentence of
condemnation? And we indeed have been condemned justly, for
we are getting what we deserve for our deeds, but this man has
done nothing wrong." Then he said, "Jesus, remember me when
you come into your kingdom." He replied, "Truly I tell you, today
you will be with me in Paradise." (Luke 23:33–43)

There is a tendency at the end of things to look back over our
shoulder and say something about what they meant. At the end
of the year on college campuses, we dress up our graduates in the

finest nylon robes we can buy and march them across a stage to get a piece of paper. When you dissect it like that, it sounds more than a little strange, but for those who have done the work, put up with the schedule, and spent the hours in the library, that odd little ritual will mean a lot. Because it will signal the end. And the strange thing about human thinking is that you usually can't tell what something was about until you get to the end. We tend to be so wrapped up in whatever it was that we can't really figure out what we think about it until it is over. Finished. Complete.

And here, we've come to an end of sorts. Not just the end of this book of sermons, but the end of the Christian year. The last Sunday of Pentecost. The close of our story before we start telling it all over again with an unmarried pregnant teenager and her nobody-carpenter of a boyfriend.

And we call this part of the story "Christ the King" because we want everyone to know how the story ends. What it meant. What it was about. Not just to remember what is long gone, but to look forward to a tomorrow yet to come. This is one of those endings that is also a beginning, where we simultaneously look backward into the story we have just come through and forward into the future we claim.

So, here at the end, what is left to say? What can we tell about this Jesus, this healer and Savior and friend and teacher, that hasn't already been told? What does it mean to proclaim this Christ as our king? We have kings for hamburgers, kings for smoothies, kings for pop music, but surely we don't mean to put Michael Jackson and Jesus in the same boat. Maybe Christ is more like the kings of history. Henry VIII and all those guys. But if he is a king of *that* kind, he sure doesn't act like it. Sometimes we wish he would, imagining Jesus just showing up and acting like the bold leader we need, claiming our enemies as his enemies, telling us exactly what to do, drawing some clear lines around what is right and wrong. We wish he would show up and give us some answers, some direction, as a good king should.

And we are not alone in that. The world Jesus entered into 2,000 years ago was much like ours in that the people were broken by fear, and mired in their own uncertainty. They wanted someone who could change the course of history, turn the tide in their favor, lead them into battle against all the doubt and brokenheartedness and frustration they had become surrounded by. They wanted a hero. A leader. A revolution. A king.

And we are just as hungry for that kind of Jesus. We want a God who's powerful. We want Jesus to look and act like a mighty leader. Everybody knows what a king does, what a king acts like, what kind of a change a king makes. So when this man comes along, the one who is supposed to sit on the throne of thrones and rule over all the nations, it seems as if there has been a major mistake. The shipping department in heaven got their memos crossed or something, because this . . . this is not what we asked for. There are no beautiful robes, no castles, no triumphant processions, not even any trumpets. In fact, the closest Jesus ever comes to any of that is riding into town on the back of a "borrowed" donkey, with some kids waving palm branches they tore off some poor tree. We at least want a king with his own donkey. But this, this is flat out unimpressive. It's not at all convincing. It is *not* what we asked for. And it is that kind of disappointment, the kind of anger that comes when you feel that you have been swindled out of something you really hoped and lived for, that leaves Jesus, this pathetic excuse for a king, hanging on a tree near Golgotha.

They also called it the Skull, and it doesn't take a lot of imagination to guess why. Jerusalem's first-century version of the landfill, a convenient place to execute criminals of all kinds. Those who had broken laws by murdering or stealing or both, and today, one who had broken hearts by not meeting expectations. Even as they nail him to a cross they keep testing him. "If he's done all these things they say he has, let's see him get out of this!" They yell it to mock him in front of the crowd, but deep down, it is a statement about hope. "Please get out of this. Show us that there is more. Prove us wrong. Do the impossible. There is still time to act like you're supposed to. Still time for a big finish . . ."

But nothing happens. Even one of the criminals there tries to get him started—"If you're the Messiah, turn this around—be worthy of our hope!" But nothing happens.

And into that nothingness, the smell of waste and death saturating the air, the cries of anger and loss piercing our ears, the dark shadows of hopelessness cast everywhere, a king is made. Not with trumpets or processionals. There are no chariots. There will be no crown other than the twisted briars pulled down over his head. There will be no throne other than these two trees tied together by the executioner. There will be no coronation ceremony besides his own murder.

But be sure, this is a king after all. For in the face of the darkest depths of humanity, sitting there squarely in the rage of the bloodthirsty and the tears of the brokenhearted, he whispers something that births a kingdom impervious to armies, ignorant of borders, and timeless in ways that history cannot measure.

"Forgive them."

In the face of hate, this one brings love. In the face of ending, this one brings beginning.

The cross should remind us of something. God's kingdom comes not in fire or cannons or angels or explosions—it comes in the power to love beyond measure. To forgive the unforgivable, to remember the forgotten, to hope for the impossible. To follow this unlikely king, born in a feeding trough and now dying on a cross— this unlikely shell of a man who is more of a king than we could have imagined or expected, more than we could have seen.

We come now to the end. And here at the finish, it is time to say what this was all about. To say that we are surrounded on all sides by a God who surprises and confounds us with the depth of an unlikely love. To hail this unlikely king whose throne is an empty cross, who calls not just the strong or the weak or the powerful but *all* to be his people, who erases the boundaries of his kingdom one heart at a time.

And like most endings when Jesus is involved, it is also a sort of beginning. Just as the balloons wither and the curtain falls and the confetti is swept away, we hear the cries of a child, unexpected and unwelcome, with no place to belong. It is time to start again. To make our way back into the story—back through the birth pangs, through the desert, through the miracle, and through the hurt—trusting that, as far as God is concerned, even familiar ground is sacred ground, and no less prone to shake with new life. This story still has something to say.

So take your place. Everything is about to begin.